Paperback: ISBN 978-1-7355794-0-5
Ebook: ISBN 978-1-7355794-1-2
Audiobook: ISBN 978-1-7355794-2-9

Editors: Robin Larin at robineditorial.com and Meaghan Minkus at https//reedsy.com/meaghan-minkus

Cover Photography: Lorraine Martin
Cover Art: Juliana Miller at Julesmarionart@gmail.com
Interior Design: Katie Anne Taylor at KatieAnneTaylor.com
Photography: Robin LaVonne Hunt

Printed with love in the United States of America
First edition

Dedication

To the families in the trenches of fostering who are weary and wonder if they can continue this fight: May you be encouraged and realize that you are loved, you can do hard things, and you are making a difference in the life of each child. It is worth it, and you need to take care of yourself too.

To the families who will begin the journey after reading this book: You can do this. Be brave. The trial is worth the blessing!

To the supporters who pray for foster children's and families' needs: Thank you for seeing us. We need you! May this book show you how you can pray and offer practical support.

To the scared caller who didn't know whether you should contact social services about a situation: Thank you for being brave enough to make that call.

To the caseworkers, GALs (guardian ad litem), CASA (court-appointed special advocate) workers, counselors, teachers, extended family, and friends who nurture, love, and advocate for all our children: You make a difference. Whether our children know it or not, you have been pivotal in helping them move beyond their trauma. They love you more than you know.

To those of you who were foster children or grew up in similar situations: May you know that you are not alone. You are loved and you do not need to feel ashamed. It was not your fault. Sometimes parents love you but cannot see beyond their own problems. You have a God who was with you in all of the scary times, and he loves you.

To family! To the children in our house who worked together to make dinner and clean up afterward so they could play outside on the evenings when I sat and wrote this book. To family and friends who treated our foster children like our other kids. Thank you for loving them and showing them healthy relationships.

To my husband, Jerry, my partner on this journey: Thank you. You make sure the kids get to piano lessons and youth group and always find time to laugh and play with all our kids.

To friends! So many of you spent time reading and offering suggestions on this project. Hugs and warm thank-yous to each of you! An extra big hug goes out to Kasey, even though she'd rather have a plant than a hug. That girl edited my book when it was my messy and emotionally raw journal, and then again after I reorganized it into topics. She helped me read the whole thing aloud twice, rewriting and throwing away thousands of words because, apparently, I'm supposed to let the readers do some of the work themselves.

To teamwork. All of your combined efforts shine through this book as you chose to share in this trial-blessing of foster care. Just the thought of encouraging those of you who touch the lives of children motivates me to step up to the battle lines of action and prayer for you. Thank you for lightening my load. I am so grateful to fight for these precious children alongside you.

To the God who is my strength: You sent people to pray for me and offer expertise and time as they read this book. Thank you for your inspiration and giving me wisdom in this process.

Breathing through Foster Care

A Survival Guide Based on
the Reflection of a Foster Mom

Robin LaVonne Hunt

Table of Contents

Preface

I wrote this book through tears with a deep contentment, knowing that I am exactly where I need to be and that God does not waste pain. Some deep truths can only come through pain, and now I can see the world in a new way through the lens of God's mercy.

There were several elements that led my husband, Jerry, and I to foster, but I don't remember what specifically inspired us to finally enroll in foster care classes. When our oldest daughter was two years

old and our son was five months old, we got our state license and began fostering. I wish that I had found books about foster parenting and knew foster families when we started years ago. The social media era was new at the time, and no one had smartphones yet. I had a million questions!

When we began our journey, we lived in a nine-hundred-square-foot, three-bedroom home, but after a year we moved to a two-thousand-square-foot, five-bedroom home. In the first two years, we fostered over twenty children. Some of them came to us by way of giving other foster parents a break for a weekend or a week. Others were placements where we said yes to children moving in indefinitely, which included everything from a toddler we had for three hours to an eleven-year-old we adopted and made a permanent part of our family.

Many years have passed since that time, and our adopted daughter is now twenty-four and living on her own. Our other children are now seventeen, sixteen, and twelve. We took an eight-year break from fostering when we adopted our daughter, and I went back to work after being a stay-at-home mom for eight years after our first baby was born. Life was busy.

Jerry has always been helpful and a wonderful dad to all of our children. When we returned to fostering, I was juggling teaching full time and a larger family. Jerry's help was as good as ever, but I still found myself desperately grasping for a lifeline of inspiration and hope. All I could think was, *Maybe I'm not strong enough to foster anymore. Maybe I need antidepressants.*

I felt so alone and overwhelmed. I found myself numbly driving to the library after school one day in search of a few minutes to myself before returning home to my houseful of kids.

I dropped to a metal stool between the aisles in the nonfiction section as I held the tiny handful of books on foster care. When I flipped to a chapter about foster kids leaving, I discovered that I was in the grief cycle and that it is normal to feel moody, melancholy, and numb as my foster children's departure neared.

I devoured others' stories and thought, *They are fighting this good fight too. Look at these people—their stories aren't organized or pretty, but they are making a difference. We're doing okay in our mess.* I needed to hear other people's stories! Reading how others worked through their struggles inspired me.

It was such a relief to realize that what I felt was normal. Just knowing that fact made me feel a little better. *It is not only okay but healthy to be sad for a while. Some parts of fostering are just plain hard, but I can do hard.* As my mom always says, "You can do anything for a little while."

I needed more stories about this hard journey. I felt like the books I read skimmed over the alarming parts of foster care or minimized them, as if the authors were afraid to scare off potential foster families. But as with childbirth, I'd rather know the hard parts so that I'm ready when they come. I want to be able to brace myself for the painful times, knowing they are just a part of the process.

If other people can go through this expression of love, I can too. Everyone knows birth is painful, but no one questions the joy. No one questions whether it's worth it or not.

My hope is that your foster journey awakens you to the reality of how much God loves you as your Father and how valuable your love is to a hurting child. There is no such thing as a perfect parent, so allow yourself to make mistakes and fight on. What you do matters! Be brave and love well.

May this book equip you to change the world, one child at a time.

This is a true story. Our foster children's names have been changed, and many details have been left out of this book for their privacy and anonymity.

When the
Call Comes

"For the Spirit God does not make us timid but gives us power, love, and self-discipline." 2 Timothy 1:7 NIV

Years ago, when we initially became foster parents in Iowa, we learned a few lessons.

Many Children Need Homes, but You Will Often Wait for a Child

It took a few months to get licensed as we waited for the next round of foster care classes to start and we had our home inspected. I was so excited when we got our license. I couldn't wait for our first call to help a child! I had a hard time sleeping while we waited over a month for that first call. My heart jumped in hope every time the phone rang.

When a caseworker finally called, she asked us if we would take a child who was a year older than our specified age range of three to eight. The child also had ADHD, which we had checked as one of the diagnosis that we were not comfortable with managing when our children were babies.

After talking with Jerry, I replied that we would take her because it was just for a few days, and we were so excited to finally get a call! The caseworker responded, "I'll call you and let you know when we'll move her; she isn't getting along with the children in her current home."

After two or three days of silence, I called the worker back and left a message to ask when she was planning on moving the little girl to our home. The worker never called back.

I was disappointed. Maybe the worker found another family or decided not to move her? Then one beautiful, sunny day two weeks later, I was sitting on my front steps talking to my cousin when the phone rang.

"This is Stephanie from Social Services. Are you still interested in taking the nine-year-old girl?"

"Yes. When would you like to move her?"

"We're near your house now. I'll drop her off."

Heart attack!

A feeling like winning the lottery!

Oh my goodness! She's coming!

I started pacing. I didn't know what to do.

Five minutes passed before the caseworker dropped off our first foster daughter. I hardly remember the worker introducing us before she left. I carried Deanna's black garbage bag of clothes to the room she would share with our two-year-old daughter, Shariah.

Shariah and our five-month-old baby boy, Ezra, couldn't have been happier about our new visitor. Deanna asked a thousand questions and played with the kids as we unpacked her clothes. Many of the clothes were not her size or were not appropriate for a nine-year-old.

I asked her where she got them, and she said, "I got some from the shelter, and Mark and Matt, my first foster family, let me pick out clothes at Goodwill."

It turned out that we were her fourth foster placement in the month since her mom's absence was reported to the police and she went into foster care.

After less than an hour with us, another caseworker picked Deanna up to take her to a supervised visit with her mom. When she left, we basked in the satisfying joy of having our first placement. We had never parented a nine-year-old before, but we knew we could provide a safe place for her to sleep, and we were excited to include her in our family for as long as she needed us. I had a hard time wrapping my mind around the idea that we were foster parents, just like when we became parents for the first time. We were really starting this journey. We were officially foster parents!

It Is Common to Get Calls for Children outside of Your Stated Preferences

Our next call for a placement came two weeks later. Again, the request for a three-month-old was outside of our preferred age range. The caseworker said the baby was probably going to be available to adopt, and she needed to place him in a foster-to-adopt home. Again, after talking about it, Jerry and I said yes.

However, we made it clear to the caseworker that we already had a five-month-old at home and we were not interested in adopting a baby, though we could take him until they found a permanent family.

He ended up living with us for nine months. The state workers were hopeful we would adopt him. Even though we loved Eli, we eventually had to be firm that he needed a forever family.

In the beginning, when the caseworker called us, she said, "You can come pick Eli up at the hospital. He has a broken arm and broken ribs."

My husband stayed home with the kids while I jumped in the car. My heart raced as I tried not to speed on the way to the hospital, crying as I prayed, *Lord Jesus, have mercy on him. Comfort him. Thank you for going with me. Make me strong.*

When I got to the hospital, I wiped my eyes and took a few deep breaths before I stepped out of the car. I was shaking.

I walked into the hospital and headed for his room. When I entered, I saw a tiny baby with a distended tummy and scrawny limbs. He was dressed in a diaper and a white T-shirt with the hospital's name written on it. His arm was in the tiniest little white sling I had ever seen.

"Is that his car seat?" I asked, referring to the car seat in the room.

"No. That belongs to Child Services," the caseworker said.

"Can I use it to get him home?"

"No. You'll need to get one," she stated.

The nurse added, "Did you bring clothes? The shirt belongs to the hospital. You can't take it."

Really?

I didn't even know what to say. Maybe this was routine for them, but I was shocked. *This baby boy has been through so much in the*

last twenty-four hours. It's late, we're all exhausted, and I need to get this
sweet baby home so I can start loving him and letting him know he is safe!

"Wal-Mart is open twenty-four hours. You can go get them there," one of the ladies instructed me.

I quickly learned that in foster care, people become flexible or they get out. As the saying goes, "Blessed are the flexible, for they will never be bent out of shape!"

Caseworkers can call down their list of foster families for hours, looking for someone who has space and is willing to take a sibling group, part of a sibling group, or even a single child. When children are removed from their parents after business hours, a caseworker cannot go home until the child has a place to go. Sometimes, the kids are in their office as they call around, looking for someone willing to foster them.

Caseworkers can request permission from a judge to place more children in your home than you are licensed for. This helps keep sibling groups together. One time we got a call for a sibling group of seven after a mom dropped them off at the police station and signed away her parental rights. When the caseworker said that she could get a variance from the judge if we were willing to take all of them, I asked if she read our profile. We had a three-month-old, a five-month-old, a two-year-old, and a nine-year-old in our three-bedroom, nine-hundred-square-foot home! We said no to that request, but we prayed for a suitable placement for them. Scared, hurting children need parents who are willing to take their whole sibling group after the trauma of being removed from their home.

Emergency or Short-Term Placements Often End Up Being Long-Term

Although caseworkers are well-meaning and hopeful that birth parents will complete the requirements to regain custody in a timely manner, timelines are elastic in the world of foster care. They often stretch as new concerns arise.

A couple of days after Deanna came, we were told she would probably go home by the beginning of the next week. Then we were told it would be a couple more weeks. Then, "it might be a month, but she'll go home by then for sure."

Soon, timelines and dates were no longer mentioned. Deanna lived with us for a year before we relocated across the state. She had to stay behind with a home in the community while her mom worked toward getting her back.

Jumping Back on the Treadmill

After we had more than twenty foster children in our home, we ended up adopting our first foster child, Deanna, when she was available for adoption. After adopting Deanna and giving birth to our daughter Christianna six months later, we took a break from fostering to focus on the four children God gave us. We moved to the village in Alaska where Jerry's family lived, and I returned to teaching for the first time since having children.

Deanna graduated and moved on to independence and married life near family in Iowa. Though we still had our other kids at home, we felt it was time to return to fostering. The need to help pressed upon our hearts. As we made the jump back into fostering, I struggled with apprehension about the challenges ahead. Life was still busy and complicated, and just as with the birthing experience, you're never ready to foster. You hope you'll be a good parent, though you might not know how you'll do it time-wise or financially. Somehow it all works out. As it does for families expecting a new baby, over time, fostering works out too. The difference in returning to fostering was that I already knew how hard it was going to be, and I had scars from the process of loving before.

For the mom, getting new foster children feels like jumping onto a moving treadmill. You feel a little clumsy and hope no one is watching. Oops! I tripped. It takes time to "catch up" while getting to know a new child and figuring out how to parent them.

Generally, people add one baby to their family at a time, and new parents typically get time off work! With fostering, you get one or more kids who come with regular appointments and behavior needs, and you just go to work the next day, keeping pace as if getting new children the night before was an item on yesterday's to-do list. Oh, and tomorrow's list just multiplied with making doctor appointments, getting clothes that fit, and figuring out transportation to and from school, therapy sessions, and parent visits too.

Whenever I adjust to jumping onto the moving treadmill of fostering, it feels as though the children's needs, the requirements of Child Services, and life in general have set the speed. After my legs catch up, it takes more time to come to a point where I am not out of breath. Through consistent training, though, my breathing steadies and my brain quits telling me that I have to stop because I can't do this.

I do a lot of internal coaching.

I often find myself saying, *I can do this. I know this is something we are meant to do. I am making a difference. Every child deserves to be loved and safe.*

When our kids go to school each day, I head there too. I teach first grade. Seeing growth in a struggling child as their teacher is exciting, and I'm so proud of them, but being a foster parent is that excitement and pride on steroids. Nothing compares to the deep satisfaction of knowing that you are making a difference in a child's life. It's not a quick fix, but it's a lasting contribution, guiding them toward healthy choices and habits in life and relationships.

Starting Again

When you get "the call," there is first an adrenaline rush and the pins and needles of *We are getting a child!* Then come details, details, details. *Those details aren't too scary . . . they are outside the "typical" child, but . . .*

Then the wait . . .

"We don't need to move them until the end of the month."

More waiting.

"I think I have a family member I can talk into taking them," the caseworker said on one particular call. "Would you be willing to take a four-year-old instead? I need to move her Monday."

"I have to talk to my husband and see if we can find childcare," I replied.

This was on a Friday morning. My stress was high as I tried to find childcare during my breaks at work. By 4:30 that afternoon I still hadn't found childcare, and I couldn't take Monday off because I needed to conduct parent-teacher conferences.

I called Jerry. We decided that since he had Monday off anyway, we could take the little girl and, if he needed to, my husband could take the next day off to find childcare. At 4:45 I was able to get through to the caseworker. When I told her our plan, she said, "Just a minute." There was a long pause while she spoke with someone in the background. Finally, the caseworker responded, "I think it would be better if she were with a stay-at-home parent."

Feeling frustrated after a stressful day of trying to find daycare amid teaching a class of first-graders, I replied, "I told you this morning when you called that I'm a teacher and we'd need to find childcare, but one of us stayed home with each of our children until they were in school, so I understand that it would be ideal if she had a stay-at-home mom or dad." But inside I thought, *It would have been a lot less stressful if you had decided that this morning when I told you we would need to find childcare. Arrgh!*

More waiting.

I had a sense of expectation, of suspended excitement, like in a

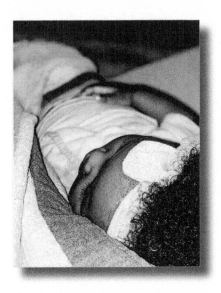

dream where you are at the top of a roller coaster in slow motion. Your eyes and heart swell as you approach the crest of the death drop, and you float in total trust and perfect peace, seeing the expanse of all that lies beyond spread out before you.

The pieces were moving into place, the perfect alignment of the children God was preparing us for, children who would be compatible with our reticent older children and our eager younger one.

It was unusual to have so many calls for kids without having them actually placed in our home. It was as if God was saving a spot at our house for kids that weren't ready to be moved yet.

2

How Will Fostering Affect My Children at Home?

"Do not be anxious about anything, but in every situation, by prayer and petition, with thanksgiving, present your requests to God. And the peace of God, which transcends all understanding, will guard your hearts and your minds in Christ Jesus." Philippians 4:6–7 NIV

We began our fostering journey when our current teens were very young. Before we began the process of reentering foster care, we had a family meeting. We explained to our birth children that they would have to be kind and patient. Foster children would need time to adjust to our home and process the loss of living without their parent or parents.

When foster children move in, they bounce between some of the stages of grief, which can include shock, denial, isolation, fear, anxiety (and upset stomachs), anger, depression, bargaining, and acceptance. Negative behaviors can emerge as subconscious cries for help or attempts to be sent home.

Our older children were open to fostering, but I could tell they were also very hesitant about the idea. They remembered what it was like when our oldest, Deanna, lived with us. When she lived at home, she was helpful, outgoing, and fun. But she was also impulsive, loved to contradict others, and argued her opinion to the death. We love her *a lot*, and she made us better parents through the challenges we experienced together. Our biological kids are much younger than she is, but they remember her getting in trouble for risky behaviors and disrespect.

My husband and I prayed. "Lord, we know you're calling us to foster again. We trust that you are going to help us have unity as a family and that you will protect our children. Prepare all of our hearts for the children you have for us."

We are a typical family in that we sink into the worlds of our individual interests. There are times when I feel as though I haven't seen our kids for most of the day. As we began to foster again, I found that it drew all of us out of ourselves and pulled us together as a family. We became more aware of the people around us. I started to see our independent, unaffectionate teens become receptive and attentive to the emotional needs of the children who became a part of our family.

It warmed my heart to see our teen son hang back when a little girl ran after him as he left the house because she wanted to go with her new brother. I started to see our son go out of his way to include this admiring little sister in his day. He became her hero.

Our teen daughter has always been quiet, independent, and, to my great sadness, tolerant of affection only when she feels like it. As she got older, she developed an aversion to younger kids in general and said she didn't like little kids. When one of our foster littles saw her lying on her tummy on the floor with a book one day, the little one lay down and threw her arm over our daughter. Our teen scooched away from the little. She wasn't comfortable with a new little kid snuggling her.

Nevertheless, like water that fills a crack and freezes to expand rock in the cold of winter, that little began to soften our teen's heart that day. It wasn't long before the little lay down on her tummy next to our daughter while she read, and our teen began to throw her arm over the little one, who snuggled in close.

Age Considerations

Although our license stated that our preferred age range was five to eighteen, when I asked our oldest daughter, Shariah, what she thought about accepting siblings who were two and six years old, she said, "That would be okay." Our youngest began praying for girls. "I really want a four-year-old little sister," she prayed.

Looking back to our initial fostering experience when our teenager was a toddler herself, I am amazed at how God is above human understanding. At the time, our foster classes taught us that it is best not to disrupt the birth order. I remember believing that we should

only adopt children younger than our birth children. It made sense, and I didn't question it in light of a popular book at the time about how birth order has a powerful impact on a child's emotions, behavior, identity, and personality development.

We never considered adopting our first foster child because she was older than our birth children. Deanna had been our foster daughter for a year when we moved across the state, and she stayed behind with hopes of going home to her birth mom. She moved in with a family who planned to adopt her if her mom's parental rights were terminated. Deanna was in all of our photo albums, and we talked about her often after we moved. We wished her the best and gave her space to bond with her new family as we adjusted to life in a new community and our oldest went off to kindergarten.

Later, we got a call from Deanna's caseworker who told us that her mom's parental rights were going to be terminated and that her current foster home was not working. We were asked three times over the course of a few months if we would adopt her. I struggled with the decision, each time more than the last. Deanna had seemed to communicate through her actions that I was not her real mom. I would feel like a terrible mom if I had a favorite child or a child I didn't love as much as the others. My husband, on the other hand, seemed as though he could be easily swayed either way, and he didn't agonize over the decision as I did.

The third time we were asked to adopt her, I was in emotional turmoil. I prayed, *Lord, I can't keep feeling guilty. You either need to make me love her the same as our birth children or stop having Child Services ask us to adopt her. Either way, Lord, we need your peace about this.*

In that instant, I heard in my mind, *Okay, it's taken care of.*

What does that mean? I thought in exasperation.

The phrase ran through my mind again: *It's taken care of.*

And then, even though I didn't understand or have an answer, I felt a peace wash over me. I knew at that moment God was going to take care of the situation. When it comes to big decisions and planning for the future, I problem-solve until I have an answer. I am usually decisive. Having peace without having found a solution didn't make sense to me. But I had peace. This had never happened to me before.

The next week, we went to a family reunion in Florida, and I spent the whole time thinking things like *Oh, Deanna would like this!* or *I wish Deanna could see this.* I was in awe when I realized that I missed her and that the attitude of my heart had shifted. I wanted her to be a part of all we were doing as a family. I missed her just as I would have missed our other kids.

When we returned from our reunion, I called the caseworker and told her that we had decided to adopt Deanna. Our other children were three and five at the time. When we told our kids that Deanna was going to move in and stay forever, they ran around the house laughing in excitement! We adopted her on Valentine's Day that year. She fit right into our family.

Only years later did I think about the birth order again. I realized that when Deanna moved in, our other kids were young enough that they did not remember her not being there. Maybe that is why it did not seem to alter their personalities or place in our family.

I do know that God can work all things together for good, even broken things. I believe that he is above birth order. If you are struggling with the decision to foster or adopt, pray for wisdom and peace in your decisions. Read your Bible and talk to people of faith you respect.

Ultimately, no one can give you the "right" answer as to whether a child should move into your home or if you should adopt a specific child. Some children you have that deep connection with, and you know you would adopt them in a heartbeat. When the decision is hard, and it might go against the opinions of those around you, lean into the peace that only God's direction can offer. No matter how much you want a child or how much you reason with yourself that you could make it work, if you don't have peace about it, don't say yes. If you are scared or feel like you don't know if you can do it, but you have a sense of peace or deep knowing that this is something you need to do, take that daring jump!

I'll never forget what I experienced when I was pregnant with our second child. We had yearned for a second baby, and as I entered the last months of my pregnancy, I had this growing fear that I would not be able to love our second baby as much as I loved our first child. If she would have let me, I could have hugged and kissed and snuggled and stared at her all day! I couldn't understand how I would be able love anyone as much as I loved her.

Yet when our son was born, I experienced the miracle of how God stretches our hearts to love beyond what we could ever think possible! With each child God has brought into our lives, he's stretched my heart a little more. It truly is a miracle. God is love, and his love is not rationed out in limited quantities. He will give us all that we need to fulfill his purposes through us when we ask. "But seek ye first the kingdom of God, and his righteousness; and all these things shall be added unto you" (Matt. 6:33 KJV).

Another Call from a Social Worker

"I'm looking for a home for two girls," the caseworker said. "I want to be up-front: they have been in three homes in the last three months. They've been in foster care before; this time they have been in foster care for a year. Recently, it's become known that the older girl was sexually abused, and the younger sister may have been as well. The recent foster dads haven't been comfortable with the older girl because she has been masturbating. She has been spending a lot of time in the bathroom at home and at school. One family said she did it while they were sitting on the couch watching a movie as a family, and another family said she did it in the grocery store."

I briefly shared our experience fostering a child who had some challenging behaviors related to the same issue. When I was a new foster mom, I had been struck with the same fears these new foster parents were feeling, but we navigated through them. This time around, I had some idea of what to expect.

"I have to talk to my husband, but I'll get back to you by Friday since you want to move the girls this weekend."

"Okay, but I'm going to continue calling around until I find a placement," the caseworker replied.

After talking and praying, Jerry and I thought we should talk to our kids. We don't usually discuss our foster children's issues with our other children, but we needed to prepare them for what they might see. Especially with an eighth-grade son, I felt that we needed to gauge his discomfort level before we moved ahead. We weren't comfortable with the behavior, but we had a sense of peace about the girls coming to live with us and felt that every child deserves a family to love them no matter what they have experienced. I knew that some abused children use masturbation as a self-soothing technique, and she needed to learn that it is not socially acceptable behavior. This behavior had more deep-rooted issues that a play therapist could help address.

That night we had a family meeting after everyone came home from work and school. We explained to our kids that the girls had moved to a couple of different homes because the oldest one had been touching her private parts, and it made the dads uncomfortable.

"So this might be something you see. She doesn't know that this is not appropriate to do in front of people. She is probably doing it as a way to process bad things she has experienced. We are not comfortable with this behavior, but she needs a family who will be patient with her while she works through what happened to her. We wanted to let you know you might see this since she did it while she was watching TV and another time in the grocery store. We don't want you to be shocked or scared about what to do. If you see it, just tell Dad or me so we can talk to her about it.

"If this is too uncomfortable for you, we do not have to take the girls, but we have also heard they can be really sweet. They need someone to love them so they don't think the things that have happened to them are their fault. What do you think? Are you open to us taking them, or does it seem like it would be too much?"

"I just don't want to share my room," our oldest daughter said. "I need my space."

"Ezra? What do you think?"

"As long as they're not boys. I don't want to share my room either."

Our youngest sat, radiating excitement that she was trying to subdue since we were having a serious conversation. "How old are they? At least I won't be the youngest anymore!" She wanted roommates.

I called the caseworker that night to let her know we were willing to take the girls. She gave us the name of the girls' current foster mom to allow us to set up a meeting. We planned to meet the next day.

Our youngest daughter, Christianna, was ecstatic that God had answered her prayers! She was not only getting two little sisters, but one of them was four, just as she had prayed! Our teens, though, were a bit hesitant to meet the girls. As we drove to meet them, we prayed that God would bless our visit. After we arrived and everyone was introduced, the kids began running around the playground.

Initially, I could tell the foster mom was nervous about meeting us when we approached her. She really loved the girls, but she said that they were more than she could handle. The foster mom gave me background information about the girls while the kids laughed and ran around. Then she said what I was thinking: "They already look like they're all siblings." Not because they looked alike—they didn't—but because they acted like siblings.

Before we parted, the mom said she was relieved to meet us and learn we were Christians. It made her feel better about the decision she had made to let the girls go to another family. "They love to go to church and pray. God is going to use them," she shared.

As we left, I asked our kids, "So what did you think of the girls?"

Our older daughter, Shariah, said, "They just felt like cousins."

"Yeah," Ezra added.

That was a very high compliment coming from them, since their cousins on both sides of the family were their best friends. For years, our children spent their school years with one set of cousins and their summers with the other cousins. They always picked up playing and talking right where they left off when they saw each other again.

I felt a sense of total peace and excitement for what God was going to do as we left that meeting. Of all the foster kids we had, I had never experienced such a smooth and comfortable initial meeting. They did feel like nieces somehow. I was amazed by how God orchestrated it so perfectly. I knew we would figure out the rest as we went. I found I wasn't nervous anymore. I was excited for the girls to move in.

Notes from My Journal: The Story Continues

The parts of the story about Ava and Madison, told in this book, came from my journal and took place over a single year.

One afternoon

"Mom, it was really cute yesterday. I was putting on my deodorant, and Ava said, 'Can I use it?' I said, 'No, it's for big kids.' And she said in a cute little voice with big eyes, 'But sharing is caring. . .' I just said, 'Let's go play upstairs with Madison,' and Ava said, 'Okay!' and she was all happy again."

A month later

I asked Ezra if eleven-year-old Madison was more annoying than his sister Christianna [whom he is very easily annoyed and angered by at times]. I've seen that he gets annoyed with Madison at times too. He replied, "She's as annoying as Christianna, but because she's not like us, it's a different type of annoying."

A week later

When I asked Christianna if she missed being the baby in the house, she said, "No, I always wanted a little sister."

She seemed to mature when the girls moved in. She didn't whine or complain about cleaning up her room, and she mentored the other girls through the same things she had struggled with up until the day before they moved in. She used to cry for up to an hour because she had to clean her room. Now when others complain, she says with a sincere face, "Come on, let's just get it done. I'll help you."

I can't help it—that makes me smile.

Another day

Christianna asked to move to the couch last night when the girls were arguing and talking late. In the morning, when she woke up, Christianna told me Madison was curled up in a blanket on the floor next to the couch. Christianna got up to go into the bedroom so Ava wouldn't be lonely when she woke up by herself. As Christianna passed through the kitchen, she smiled when she saw Ava snuggled up in her blanket on the rug in the middle of the kitchen floor. So cute.

Our Teen's Experience with Another Foster Child

After being jolted awake from a nap by a screaming tantrum, one day, our high school daughter, Shariah, emerged from her room disorientated.

"That was terrifying! It sounded like someone was dying. I know I shouldn't, but sometimes I just love tantrums. Like when Ava was screaming at her sister, who was twice her size, 'I'm bigger than you!' And that time Nathan was screaming, 'I want celery! I want celery!' after he refused to eat it at the table when you told him he could have some. Then he let out a bloodcurdling scream that made it sound like someone was attacking him, and no one was even near him."

Who knew that Shariah, who had an aversion to little kids, would love tantrums? Sometimes there were elements of humor that could lessen the stress of tantrums after they were over. I remembered how that celery incident had continued into a meltdown as Nathan got ready for bed.

"I want a story! You didn't read me a story! I don't know about God, and you won't tell me about him! Now I'm never going to learn about God! I want you to sing me a song!"

My heart raced, but I replied calmly, "If you stop screaming at me, I will pray with you. I don't read stories and sing songs for people who are screaming at me." He did calm down enough for me to pray with him, and I assured him that I would read and sing with him the next night when he asked respectfully.

I shared the following story with our teen about a recent tantrum that she would have found amusing.

After a day of his misbehaving at school, I told our foster son that we were going to talk about what had happened when we got home. He said, "I'm not going to listen because I don't like to listen to bad things." To which I replied, "I don't like hearing about bad things either, so don't do bad things at school."

"Well, I'm stronger than anybody! I'm even stronger than Hulk, so I can do whatever I want when I get mad. I'm even stronger than Spiderman!"

"Superheroes help people, and I'd like it if you helped people," I replied.

At that, he went off on a tangent about superheroes. The venom of anger seemed to drain from him as he rambled. By the time we got home, he was ready to talk about what had happened at school, and he willingly wrote a letter of apology to his teacher.

Thoughts about Fostering by Christianna When She Was Eleven

I enjoy sharing a room with my foster sisters Madison and Ava. We have fun playing together. Ava loves to swing high on swing sets because she says she wants to be tall. Madison always asks me to play pirates because she wants to go out on the sea and live on a ship. When we play princesses, Ava will be the youngest, or she wants to be the dad. Madison will be the middle child, or sometimes she wants to be the baby of the family. I will be what they want me to be because I don't want to cause a fight.

Sometimes it's hard to deal with Ava at night because she won't go to bed even when my mom tells her to lie down or to stop talking. Ava will cry for hours, or she will talk to us all night.

Madison and I are exhausted in the morning. Most of the time we tell her to go to bed and she lies down and sings or plays with her stuffies. Madison and I just ignore Ava if she talks to us. Then she goes back to doing what she was doing.

The rest of the time, she is kind. Ava is fun to play with. I like how Ava isn't scared to talk to new people. Also, it's fun to do her hair and pick out her clothes.

Madison is funny and creative. She is also a problem solver who likes challenges and adventures. When Madison doesn't want to do something, she just plays or wanders off and does her own thing. Sometimes she'll clean our room quickly when we're going to do something exciting, like watch a movie.

When Ava is cleaning her part of the room, she'll sometimes cry or say, "No! I don't want to!" Then she'll scratch, hit, spit, or punch you and then hide. But she always hides under the bed or in our closet, so we know where to find her. She mostly does that to her sister because Madison picks on her, and Madison makes it worse by hugging Ava when she's mad. Then she gets angrier and pinches Madison. Sometimes my mom will tell her again that there is no hitting, and Ava sits in time-out. She says sorry, and we all start to play again. If she's grumpy and mad, my mom tells us to go to the other room so Ava can calm down.

If I want alone time, I have to use my time after school to be by myself before one of my parents picks them up from daycare. I draw or color. It gets boring after a little while. I like to play the piano, and Madison and Ava sing along if I sing. We have a lot of fun together!

Thoughts About Fostering by Shariah When She Was Seventeen

Although I personally do not plan to ever become a foster parent, I enjoy meeting all types of people and seeing the way they change me. Foster care helped me learn how to deal with difficult personalities.

This Foster Mom's Perspective

The children who came into our home had so many different lessons to teach us. As the children shared their stories, we became grateful for the myriad of blessings we have in each other.

Foster children moved us to pray for God's rescuing power to protect them as they moved on from our home. If their presence in our family had not left tender footprints on our hearts, we would not have been moved to step up to the battle line of prayer to intercede for them. Even if pain is what it takes to make that imprint, I want that imprint. If I did not have a tender bruise, I would not be moved to pray for them.

There are foster children I barely remember. I used to feel bad that I don't pray for them regularly. I found a place of acceptance in myself that I don't often pray for all our former foster children. I realize that the ones who left a bruise on my heart are the ones I'm still assigned to. Their purpose in my life and my purpose in their lives are not done yet. I don't feel a need to reconnect with the children in person. I wish for them to be happily settled with their adoptive or birth families.

When Matt Redman's song "Blessed Be Your Name" comes on, I find myself praying with fervor, and sometimes tears fill my eyes at the memory of a baby boy who lived with us fifteen years ago.

I knew that his needs were more than I could handle. He was the one everyone thought we would and should adopt. I knew I couldn't, though I desperately wanted him. My heartstrings are sometimes plucked when I see a cemetery because that is where I went when I felt as though my heart was being ripped out of my chest while I held him in desperation. I experienced anguish in his loss. But I would do it again. He is still worth it, and I am thankful for the memory of the pain. God used me to love him well. We were the bridge to his forever family as we were able to help him through his injuries, surgery, food intolerances, and some of the hard parts of his reactive attachment disorder. I am reminded of the pain at times, and I pray for him and his adopted family. Instead of assigning me to adopt him, God has assigned me to pray for him.

I will never be the same. You will never be the same after fostering. You will learn to love more deeply and give in a way that will change you and help you understand God's love for you in a profound way.

3

What Happens When a Child Comes: Getting the Call!

"Commit your work to the LORD, and your plans will succeed."
Proverbs 16:3 (CEB)

Preparing the Room

The caseworker said that Madison and Ava needed to move. We planned to have their foster mom drop them off for a couple of hours the next day to help them transition. They would officially move in the following day at 3:00 p.m.

This was really happening! We needed to get some furniture! While we were waiting for a call for foster children, we didn't know what age or gender the kids would be, so we hadn't gotten beds yet. The arrangement would need to be different based on the room or rooms they would share with our kids. We decided to have kids younger than our own children this time around since our children were getting older.

We figured that with the girls coming, a bunk bed with a bunky board that slid in and out would be the best option. A bunky board doesn't pop up like a trundle; it's a little over an inch off the ground and a regular mattress can fit on it. It has wheels that make it easy for a four-year-old to push under the bunk beds each morning if she sits down on her bottom and shoves it in with her feet.

Buying new furniture was expensive initially, but we were able to find some deals. We needed a bunk bed, two twin mattresses, the bunky board, all the bedding, and a couple of dressers to get started. There weren't any used bunk beds or small dressers listed online at the time. We heard about a secondhand store that had wooden bunk beds from the local army base. They were sturdier than the ones we saw at Wal-Mart and half the price!

We went through Christianna's things to make room for two more girls in her room. We moved our daughter's single bed out and moved in dressers and mattresses, then put together the bunk bed. We put the two girls' dressers side by side in the closet so they'd have more room to play.

A couple of teacher friends asked if they could do anything to help us get started. One gave each of the girls a blanket for her bed, and the other gave us enough money to pay for most of the bunky board. It encouraged me to see how supportive these teachers were as we began this adventure. When they asked periodically how the girls were doing, I was able to share some of the little joys and prayer needs as we began the process of coming together as a family.

The caseworker wanted the girls to continue at their daycare as they transitioned to our home. Since our house would be the girls' third home in three months, it made sense to let them continue preschool and daycare with friends and teachers they already knew. The daycare was excellent, but the monthly fee was $200 above the daycare allowance the state pays. We had to make a payment before our first stipend came. I figured that once the girls adjusted, we could always transition them to a daycare fully covered by the childcare allowance if we needed to.

Outfitting a child or two with quality boots, coats, hats, gloves, and other clothes is pricey. We found a local children's secondhand store to be helpful more than once. Kids lose hats and gloves! Our foster clothing discount card for ten to twenty percent off at local stores was useful too.

Some foster families keep totes of different-sized clothes and gear on hand for future foster children. I did this with our biological children as the older kids outgrew their clothes. I kept the newer clothes in labeled totes for the younger kids to grow into—one color of tote for girl clothes and another color of tote for boy clothes, labeled by size.

When we were new to foster care, we had a lot of short placements with a broad age and size range (three-month-old to eleven-year-old boys and girls). We only had two long-term situations that lasted over six months; the clothing totes came in handy then.

As I grow older, I crave simplicity, and the placements we accept have become a little more predictable. Now I keep only one tote of clothes that includes items I picked up on clearance and previous foster kids' clothes they outgrew. Extra socks, unisex T-shirts or shorts, and clearance items for girls a little younger than our youngest are a safe buy since we are most likely to say yes to foster girls who will share a bedroom with our youngest. She always wants to share her room.

Memory of Foster Children Moving In by Christianna When She Was Eleven

Before [Ava and Madison] came, I was wondering what they would be like, what their personalities would be like, and what types of things they would like to do. I wondered if they enjoyed the same things as me. How tall would they be? And what would they look like? It was all a mystery until I met them.

We met at a playground. When we got there, the adults introduced us, and Madison asked if we wanted to play tag. It was so much fun! Ava asked if she could tag us, and we said yes.

Then they came to play at our house to get used to us. We showed Madison and Ava our room where they were going to stay, and we showed them around the house.

After coming over to play, they brought all their stuff to our house. Their foster mom had to leave, so we prayed with her. We prayed about her being strong and having patience while she was waiting for her next foster kids. When we were praying, Madison was crying, but Ava was looking around at everything. The moms were crying. Then they gave each other hugs. I don't know why my mom was crying, because she wasn't leaving. Their foster mom talked to Mom for a while. I hugged Madison, and we started playing.

Reflections as a Mom

After the girls visited our house, I called and talked to their foster mom about how it went. She was surprised that they were excited about coming back the next day. After having the girls for two months, I could tell this was very hard for her. She was attached.

She told me that the girls were probably going to ask us pretty quickly if they could call us Mom and Dad. She mentioned that they wanted to be part of a settled family. On my end, it felt good to know the girls were coming from a foster couple who loved and cherished them. The mom said they would continue to pray for the girls.

Ava and Madison were very excited when they arrived to move in. Their foster mom was trying to hold back her tears. Jerry and Ezra helped her bring in the girls' totes. She quickly gave the girls hugs and told them she loved them and they were going to be happy in their new home. She said we could have the booster seat that the youngest used too. The girls started crying when they saw her emotion and gave her lots of hugs and kisses as we prayed, and then she made her escape. She forgot to leave the booster seat but came back and left it when the girls wouldn't see her.

The girls came with so many totes of clothes, shoes, and toys. It was overwhelming. One of them had three winter coats and the other had two. The foster mom said that many of the clothes were from different foster homes, and not all of them were appropriate for them. If things were a measure of love, these girls were well loved! I went through and picked out the women's clothes and the boy's clothes that they wouldn't wear. The girls were all bows, tutus, and sparkles. In case I hadn't noticed, the oldest foster daughter, Madison, clarified, "We're girly girls."

I let Madison and Ava pick out their favorite clothes to save. I told them they could keep as many clothes as their dresser and closet would hold. They filled their dressers and two rods in the closet with dresses, sweaters, vests, and coats. They filled two totes and a small bookshelf with their favorite toys and books. They still had multiple totes of toys and clothes left over that didn't fit in the room. I had them each choose their seven favorite stuffed animals for their beds, and I explained they were going to share with kids who didn't have as many toys and clothes. They traded a couple of stuffies out before they decided they were ready to share the rest.

I wasn't sure what the protocol was for handling foster children's things, so I left a couple of messages with the caseworker to see if she wanted to pick them up. Their mom didn't have a home at the time. The caseworker never responded, so after talking to the girls, we donated them.

Helpful Tips

If a foster parent drops the foster children off, you can stop by Child Services and pick up a medical consent form if the caseworker hasn't dropped it off within twenty-four hours. Because the state has legal custody of foster children, the caseworker's signature gives a foster parent consent for children to receive medical care. Caseloads are usually so large that I try to help by picking up the consent form myself. Caseworkers are supposed to lay eyes on the child at least once a month, but these timelines stretch when caseloads are unreasonably large and workers are dealing with urgent situations.

My experience is that if a caseworker drops off a child, they usually stay for about five to fifteen minutes to help the child adjust and to answer any questions. Since we have other kids in our home, the caseworker or I will sometimes say, "You kids get to know each other while the adults visit in the other room." Even if the kids are all staring at each other awkwardly when we leave them, they are often laughing or playing in no time. I've found that kids in the home help new children figure out how things run by example and candidness.

While I have a few minutes with the caseworker, I state concerns and ask any additional questions. Before the worker comes, it helps to write questions down so I don't forget amid the excitement and anxiety of a new child in the home. If there is a specific concern you want the caseworker to discuss with the child, they can be an excellent backup in setting expectations before they leave. For example, some homes are technology-free, and children go by the house rules. At our house, we have all our children's passwords for their devices. We also have a monitoring app that will alert us if a child is looking at or typing something questionable.

You do not have to give children access to things you are not comfortable with, even if a caseworker says a child can do something. For example, I was not comfortable when a caseworker said a child could call and talk to his mom after 7:00 p.m. Be up-front with caseworkers in situations like this and let them know if you do not want to be responsible for supervising calls with parents. In general, I am more comfortable with children talking to their siblings on the phone than their parents. At times, I have allowed children to call their parents when I get to know the kids and the parents and I am comfortable with the situation. I find that allowing children or parents too much access to each other causes mood swings of anger and sadness that translate into tantrums and defiance. Finding this communication balance becomes a bit of a dance. Of course, visits with parents are essential because reunification is the goal. Some foster parents are more comfortable interacting with birth parents than others, and each situation is different.

When children come, introduce yourself and let the child know what they can call you. I generally say with a welcoming smile, "Hi! I'm Robin. I'm the mom here, so you can call me Robin or Mom. I'll answer to either name." This is an important time to be welcoming and warm because children are scared when they come. I want to allow children to feel comfortable by giving them permission to call me Mom or my name. This is a sensitive issue, and I found that many kids didn't call me anything until I gave them some options. When children don't feel like they have any control over their lives, they like to be given a few real choices.

I state, "You are safe here. We do not hurt each other in our house or call each other names. If we get mad at each other, we talk to each other about it, and we expect you to learn to do the same thing. This house is a safe place." When necessary, we explain that the person who hurt them is in jail or does not know where we live.

We show a new child where they can put their things. Then we ask if they are hungry before we give them a tour of the house. We've found that most kids are very respectful when they come. While they do not know our family's boundaries, they ask permission to do things that are important to them.

One ten-year-old boy asked, "Do kids in your house get to play games with guns? I have some games with guns." I said, "No. Can I see what games you have?" He got them for me, and I told him I would give them to the caseworker to give to his parents, which we did. It

wasn't as easy to have him give us his phone. Kids in our home don't have phones until they are fifteen. In addition to this family guideline, we require that all visits with parents be supervised. He was sneaking calls to his parents, who were telling him he didn't have to go to school. I explained that the phone was still his and he would get it back when he left, or I could give it to the caseworker to give to his parents. I also reassured him he would get to talk to his parents when he had a supervised visit.

We explain expectations as the opportunity arises the first time so we don't overwhelm kids amid trauma and change. For example, we might say, "Wash your hands; it's time for dinner." When they come to the table, we say, "Pick a seat. We eat dinner together as a family every day. If someone isn't hungry, we all still sit together and visit while others eat. Once dinner is done, we don't get it out again later." This type of discussion, when everyone is on common ground before an incident arises, helps prevent conflict in the future.

Another example is, "We all work together to keep our house clean so we have time to do fun things. When kids in our family turn nine, they start learning how to do dishes. They get to pick their day.

What day would you like? Everyone cleans their room, puts their things away around the house, and does one other job." Sometimes kids suggest a job they like to do, and other times I give them suggestions of things they could do. A preschooler could feed the dog, put away silverware when it's clean, or help set or clear the table. Younger elementary kids could set the table, help make dinner, sweep, fold towels, or deliver clean laundry after it's folded. Older kids could make a meal one night a week, plan school lunches for the week, make the shopping list of items needed for the lunches, take the dog for a walk each day, vacuum, sweep, clean their bathroom, or fold laundry. These are ideas we have suggested to kids in our home. Kids pick only one of these jobs to do regularly.

To keep things simple, our kids do the same job indefinitely until they request a job change. Just like the working world, it is easier for a job to become a habit instead of having to decide what they want to do each day. If I notice that a task seems too hard or causes frustration, I will ask the child if they would like to switch to a more appropriate job.

Sometimes we need to explain expectations outside the home too. When a high schooler moved in with us, I explained that sometimes we run into our foster children's parents at the grocery store. If that happens and you want to say hi to them or hug them, you can. Or, if you would rather not talk to them, you can stay by us, and we do not have to go near them.

Fostering, like all parenting, is an art. You figure it out as you go, but it gets easier as you develop your technique. It won't always be pretty, and you will mess up. We're all doing the best we can, so forgive yourself and move on if something didn't come out right. Ask your kids to forgive you for not responding the way you should have, and be intentional about being prepared to act differently if a similar situation arises again.

4

Addressing Challenges in Parenting Foster Kids

"So, chosen by God for this new life of love, dress in the wardrobe God picked out for you: compassion, kindness, humility, quiet strength, discipline. Be even-tempered, content with second place, quick to forgive an offense. Forgive as quickly and completely as the Master forgave you. And regardless of what else you put on, wear love. It's your basic, all-purpose garment. Never be without it."
Colossians 3:12–14 (MSG)

In the daily living and giving of fostering and parenting, you will find that you will develop gifts, attitudes, and systems that will make the journey a little easier as you go. Your ability to endure higher noise levels, tantrums, and negative behaviors will increase and your ability to be fair and straightforward with your responses will develop too.

Years ago, as a new teacher, I struggled with children's negative behaviors. I had heard that children feel safe when they know where the boundaries are, but I didn't know how to create that environment. There were two amazing teachers in the classrooms on either side of me. One explained to me a few times that I needed to be consistent. If a student thinks they might be able to do something once every twelfth time, they will keep trying to do it in case this is the twelfth time, or if I'm too tired to enforce the boundary. At the time, this consistency seemed so unforgiving. I wondered if I could maintain this high standard.

I became more consistent in addressing behaviors, and I discovered that the more challenging a child is, the more everyone benefits from routine. If everyone does homework after school or reads for half an hour after dinner, for example, it is one less argument to deal with once the habit is learned. That is just what happens every day. Distracted children benefit from having a special spot to accomplish a task. Limit distractions and tension with others in the house by providing a special place for a child to accomplish a task: a cushion, a little nook, or a spot around a corner can work.

My classroom aide, Lillian, was an incredible and lasting influence on my ability to get kids moving in the direction I need them to go. Everyone always loved her. She often reminded me not to be so serious. I discovered that by letting go and allowing myself to have fun with kids, I could get a lot farther than when I tried to keep pushing through what needed to be done each day. Start with a smile and let people know that you like them for who they are and that you notice what they are good at and what they enjoy doing.

I'll never forget one little guy in my first-grade class, Lawrence. He was tiny, and he loved to run. He was very proud of the fact that he was fast! Acknowledging his speed filled him with pride and gave us a connection that helped when he needed correction.

The concept of seeing the value in others applies to all people, but I think it is especially vital for foster children who have been stripped of many parts of their family, culture, and identity. They need to have something they can be proud of, a part of them they can own in a world where people and security are not certainties in their lives.

In Alaska, many Native children who enter foster care have to adjust to a different culture in the city with different food and social expectations. When I lived in a village for ten years, a caseworker told me that there was only one foster family in our school district for a few years. And our school district was the size of Ohio geographically. Foster children take one to three different planes to get from their isolated villages of less than a thousand people to Fairbanks, with a hundred thousand people, or Anchorage, with over a quarter million people. This is the equivalent of sending these children to another country. More foster homes are needed in rural Alaska.

Navigating Our Own Challenges

When Madison came to live with us, she was an outright hoarder. Everything was vitally important to her. When I tried to help her clean her room, I couldn't throw away the gum wrapper or the strand of yarn that came off her sweater because she was going to use them to make something.

For weeks after Madison and her sister came, the contents of their dressers and toy totes emptied onto the floor each day. There were a lot of tears and temper tantrums as I helped the girls clean up. I realized that having less stuff would make it easier for them to pick up after themselves.

We went from two totes of toys to one. Honestly, I don't know why they took everything out every day. The only things Ava played with were her Mega Blocks and one doll. And Madison liked to draw and write stories in her sketch pad or read her Bible.

To help with the hoarding, we made a rule that if anyone brought something into the house, we must get rid of a similar item. I gave

Madison an art box. Anything she wanted to keep for art projects had to fit in the box. If the box didn't close, then she needed to get rid of something. This helped limit the art supplies that could be misinterpreted as garbage.

On the flip side of their desire to keep everything was the girls' appreciation for things that were given to them or done for them. Both girls would regularly say, "Thank you, Mom, for dinner."

It is important to allow kids to choose what they want to keep because the items might be connected to something familiar or someone they love. A cheap, broken necklace might have been a gift from someone special. Since they have no control over many aspects of their lives, these are opportunities when they can decide what they get to keep.

Though foster children become attached to their belongings, I have noticed a frustrating pattern. They are often rough with their things as well as other people's things. They are used to getting clothes, furniture, and other supplies for free or handed down. To battle this thinking or behavior, I talk about the importance of taking care of what we own.

When they moved in, our foster daughters shared a room with our youngest daughter, and we had the girls lie down at 8:00 p.m. On a good night, Ava talked nonstop until she fell asleep around 10:00 p.m. We could not find a way to get her to stop talking, no matter how much the older girls complained they couldn't sleep. My husband and I spoke to Ava, offered incentives, and enforced consequences, but Ava wouldn't stop talking.

On bad nights, which outnumbered the good at times, Ava cried or screamed until she fell asleep between 11:00 p.m. and 1:00 a.m. Some nights she would holler over and over, "I want to play outside!" or "I want to watch a movie!" When Ava incorporated hitting and kicking her sisters into this bedtime routine, or when they asked for relief, we let the older girls sleep in the living room.

Another difficult issue foster families will inevitably have to deal with is sibling jealousy. One day Madison said, "That's not fair. You get to go to store with Mom," and another time, "How come she got a donut?"

Our older daughter said, "It all evens out. Sometimes you get to go with Mom, and I don't. When you're with Mom, you stop and get a treat sometimes when we aren't there."

When we do stop somewhere fun, I coach the kids, saying that if they take food into the house and the others ask them if they can have some, they need to share.

"If you don't want to share it, finish it before you go into the house. If anyone asks where we went, tell the truth, but don't tease or brag about it."

Notes from My Journal: The Story Continues

One day after school

I got a note from Madison's teacher. Madison had been going to the bathroom in the nurse's office so the nurse could make sure she was not camping out in the bathroom, masturbating. Madison said the nurse was gone when she had to go to the bathroom today, so she went to the regular bathroom, but I guess she was in there for a long time.

I asked her why she was in the bathroom for so long today. Was she touching herself? She started to cry. I asked if she knew why she did it. Did she do it when she was lonely or because it felt good? She said she didn't know why. I asked if she had done it at our house, and she said no. She hadn't been in the bathroom for long periods at home, but I didn't know if it was something she did in bed at night.

I explained to Madison that she already missed a lot of class time since Child Services took her out of school three times a week to visit her mom and see a counselor. When she was at school, she needed to be in class, learning. We prayed together and I told her God loves us the same no matter what we do. There was nothing we could do to make him like us less or to make him love us more.

Later that week

After school, when I came into the kitchen, Madison was already home. Jerry had picked the girls up from daycare.

"Hi, Madison," I said as I came into the kitchen. She was pouring herself a glass of water.

"Hi, Mom. I didn't like it when you pushed me yesterday." She looked right at me.

I felt as though the wind got knocked out of me.

"When did I push you?" I said, trying not to sound defensive.

"Last night."

"Show me where we were and what we were doing." My heart beat rapidly. I would never intentionally hurt a child!

"We were standing right here, and you pushed me and told

me to go to bed." She gestured in front of the sink. The memory of what she was talking about dawned on me.

"Madison, when you say I pushed you, it sounds as though I was trying to hurt you. Do you think I was trying to hurt you?"

"No."

"If you say I pushed you, people will think I was trying to hurt you. I asked you to go to bed six times last night, and you were not listening to me. If any of the kids in the house were not listening, I would do the same thing. I put my hand on your back and said, 'Let's go. It's time for bed,' as I directed you toward your room. I'm glad we talked about this, Madison. If someone is hurting you, you need to tell someone, but you can't make it sound like people are hurting you if they aren't, or they could get in a lot of trouble." I pushed down the rising frustration and fear.

I sought out support from Madison's play therapist by sharing the incident with her. She explained that children who have had traumatic experiences can project those incidents onto innocent interactions in the present. For example, when I was guiding Madison toward the door with my hand on her back, she perceived it as a push.

That explanation was frightening to me! I did not want to be accused of being abusive. The play therapist explained that I could talk about the situation aloud to help her process what was happening.

After that, I started narrating as I corrected her little sister. "I asked you to go to bed, and you refused. I told you I would carry you if you didn't walk." When her sister threw a fit and started kicking and hitting me, I stated, "You are hurting me. I'm not hurting you. You are okay. I'm trying to help you get to bed."

Two days later

After dinner, I helped the girls pick up their clothes, and little Ava acted happy. One of the girls folded a shirt for her and said nicely, "Put this in your shirt drawer."

Ava turned and spit on her angrily!

I said sternly, "We do not spit on people."

She turned and gave me the ugliest look of intense hatred and spit on me! Then she started yelling at me at the top of her voice that she did not want to clean her room.

"I will not talk to you when you are yelling at me," I said. I deposited Ava in a chair at the kitchen table and set the timer for four minutes. Twenty seconds into the time-out, the four-year-old began sweetly singing, "Yes, Jesus loves me. Yes, Jesus loves me."

Months later

It was so good to have my mom visit from out of state. She asked, "How can Ava wake up angry every day? The day hasn't even started yet."

She turned to Ava and said, "Ava, let's go have a special talk, just us girls." Afterward, my mom told me they talked about waking up happy, and she gave Ava a special name. After that, when Ava's grumpy mood popped up throughout the day, my mom began calling Ava "Sunshine." Surprisingly, Ava switched right back to her cheerful self. It was truly magical! I had seen her go from happy to angry in an instant, but I didn't know she could switch back to cheerful just as fast.

One morning, as usual, Ava was the first kid in the house to wake up. She stomped upstairs, crying her way angrily through the house. When she arrived upstairs, I asked, "What's wrong?" She stopped crying to whine, "I'm tired!"

"Where is the sunshine, Miss Ava Sunshine?"

"Look, Mommy, I'm happy now." She smiled at me through her tears. She came over for a hug and said, "I love you, Mommy!"

"I love you too." I dropped a kiss on her adorable little forehead, and she beamed lovingly up at me.

Every once in a while, someone offers a piece of seemingly magical advice, and the "Sunshine" nickname was it for Miss Ava. This worked most of the time as she started her day.

Two days later

The caseworker came to do a home visit. We all worked together to clean the house before she arrived. The visit seemed positive. I asked if she wanted a tour, but she didn't seem particularly interested, so she had a seat at the kitchen table. She asked how the girls were doing. I told her some of their interests and talked a little about recent behaviors that we have shared with the counselor, including the ongoing sleep struggles.

I shared our ongoing frustration with the play therapist, she mentioned that it is not uncommon for children who have experienced trauma to have a hard time going to sleep. Sometimes this is because bad things happened to them when they were sleeping, or sometimes they are afraid of having bad dreams about things that have happened.

Then the therapist offered us a lifeline. "Some parents have found melatonin to be helpful."

After researching melatonin for children, we looked for it in the supplement aisle of the grocery store and bought a bottle.

Ava chewed her supplement thirty minutes before bed as recommended and then *asked* if she could go to bed because she was tired. She lay down with the girls, and within twenty minutes, all of them were asleep!

After struggling with this issue for so long, this felt like a miracle! Had it really been five months of three to six hours of drama each night? I just thought it was part of her trauma, the fact that she was outgrowing naps, and that she was strong-willed and had horrible temper tantrums. In hindsight, even though I had mentioned that she had a hard time sleeping at our well-child visit, I wish I had been more assertive about asking a doctor or naturopath for recommendations long ago.

Ava was happier during the day and had fewer temper tantrums because she had the rest she needed. Everyone else was happier because we weren't making trips to her room at 1:00 a.m. to tell her to be quiet.

The next day

It was another day of coaching kids to respond appropriately to conflict. After another yelling match between the girls, I drew Ava away by letting her help me get dinner ready so Madison could

finish her nightly reading for school. As we ripped up lettuce, I talked to Ava about letting her sister get her homework done.

At the end of Madison's reading time, I went in to talk to her about the incident.

"Is your book good?" I asked.

"Yeah. I like these graphic novels. Our school library has a lot of these," she replied.

"So far, you have remembered to read on your own two times this week. Good job! I know you don't like it when Ava bothers you when you're reading." I smiled at her. "Wow! You were really loud when you hollered at her earlier. Did it make her stop when you got loud?"

"No. She was still bothering me."

"What could you try next time she is bothering you and makes you mad?"

"I could tell her to stop, or I could ask her if she wants to do something like play outside with Christianna," Madison responded.

"What if she doesn't want to and continues to bother you? What else could you do?"

"I could move somewhere else or tell you or Dad if she follows me."

"I'm so glad you know what to do. I can't wait to see you try one of those ideas next time Ava bothers you," I replied.

It was so good to hear Madison verbalize the options we were trying to teach her. Now she just needed to start putting them into practice!

Identifying Triggers and Setting Boundaries

Often, our foster girls were a trigger for each other. Our birth children have seasons when they don't get along. However, our foster daughters' therapist said they were a trigger for each other on a deeper level because they were both present during times of trauma.

Noticing triggers and times when the girls became aggressive allowed me to be intentional about avoiding negative behaviors. In our girls' case, it meant having them get ready for the day and ready for bed apart from each other and within hearing distance of an adult. When I allowed them to get up and get dressed in their room downstairs together, they would take turns hollering at each other and then stomping up the stairs to tell me that one of them stuck out her tongue, said something mean, hit, pushed, or scratched her. It helped to have Ava, who used to always wake up angry, come upstairs first thing in the morning and get ready away from her sister.

I appreciate the advice I received as a new foster mom. Long ago, when our oldest daughter moved in, she talked back and argued with everything I said. The best one-liner another parent ever gave me was "I do not argue with children." The foster mom explained that when a child was defiant, she reasoned with herself internally: *I'm the adult; I will outlast you. I'm going to win this one.*

In truth, when we choose not to argue with children, everyone wins. When we follow through with consequences, we teach children how to interact with others appropriately. They grow more pleasant to be around as they develop appropriate, healthy relationships with both children and adults.

I'm so glad I learned that when a child misbehaves, I don't have to get upset or angry to communicate that they messed up. It makes parenting a lot less stressful. When a child doesn't get the dishes done, I don't have to get frustrated. I remind them once that if they don't get the dishes done tonight, they will have dishes again tomorrow. Of course, sometimes I say, "You need to work on dishes until you get them done because we need dishes for dinner."

We discuss offenses as needed. If it is only with one child, we have the conversation privately, and it is not discussed with the other children. If everyone is involved or we have a growing problem, we have a family meeting.

One growing problem we had was the kids' habit of leaving all the lights on in the bathroom. At a family meeting, we explained that it costs money. We told the kids that if we saw all the lights on in the bathroom three times in a week and no one was around, they would all owe a third of that week's allowance to help pay for the extra electricity. A sign magically appeared on the light switch shortly afterward, and the kids posted the strikes. The light is rarely left on now.

When we have conflicts between children, each child gets to share how they have been wronged. We discuss others' rights and our expectations of respect for each other. Sometimes kids add to the discussion, and in the end, we ask if anyone needs to apologize. At times we walk kids through the process.

Say their name. Tell them what you didn't like. "You always say no when I ask to sit on your bed, and then you just sit on my bed without asking, and when I tell you to get off, you don't."

"You have to share your room, but your bed is your space. You need to ask nicely if you don't want someone to sit on your bed. If you want to sit on someone else's bed, you can ask. If someone asks you to get off their bed, you need to be respectful and get off."

I don't need to raise my voice or get angry. When an offense is over with apologies and/or a consequence served, it is over. I do not make children feel as though they are in trouble or I don't like them. It is over. I explain to children that I love them no matter what they do.

A Day in the Life
of This Foster Mom

"Now may the Lord of peace himself give you his peace at all times and in every situation. The Lord be with you all." 2 Thessalonians 3:16 (NLT)

The girls will adapt to our expectations and we will adjust to their needs.

As I tried to stifle my tears and the world turned blurry, I said to myself, *don't cry. It is going well. Really. I've been here before. It's different, but this feels cyclical somehow. Familiar, though different. Breathe in . . . breathe out . . . breathe in . . . breathe out . . .*

It wasn't just Jerry and me this time. Our children were older now, and they were going through the cycle of the emotions of foster care with us. At least they had their own rooms. They weren't as close to the raw emotions of dealing with the drama that came along with children working through loss and anger, separated from their birth families.

We are prepared for this season, I said to myself.

I'm reminded of a quote I've heard over the years: no matter how big or small, there is a difference only you can make.

Our foster girls were adorable. Madison, the older one, was artistic, thoughtful, loving, and helpful. Ava, the younger one, had a smile that melted any heart and shiny hair that attracted many compliments. "She is so adorable!" I often heard as we were out and about.

She had a charismatic sense of style. I bought the tutus, leggings, and skirts, but she was very opinionated about when and how she would wear her clothes. She was mixing prints before I knew that was a thing and wearing clothes I wasn't sure went together, but her outfits evoked many compliments around town. Ava was very affectionate and loved to ride with me or sit by me. Both girls had to have a hug and wanted to kiss my cheek every time I left for an errand or they were getting ready for bed. They loved helping me make breakfast or dinner. They fit right in with our other kids as we went for walks or they all played tag. As I have always told my children, they are gifts from above (Jas. 1:17).

Notes from My Journal: The Story Continues

One weary day

I was *exhausted!* Ava was an active four-year-old who needed to be watched. Madison was a typical eleven-year-old sister who didn't always listen to her siblings. I'd been dragging through the last couple of days uncomfortably tired. Teachers have to take courses to renew their licenses, and on Tuesday night in class, I had to stand up and walk around to stay awake.

I'd been fatigued since Spring Break. The younger three girls stayed up and had a giggle fest Monday night until 11:00 p.m. I'd been staying up too late trying to have time with our older kids, watching a TV drama together after the younger girls went to bed.

It was so good to have that bonding time, but I couldn't keep up the pace.

I was going to quit piano at the end of the month, and Shariah was too. She had been an excellent help with dinner and with the girls here and there. Recently, though, she was overwhelmed and emotional. She felt as though there were always people around now that we had two more people in the house.

Lord, help all of us to find balance.

The end of a month

It was Sunday. I wanted to take a day off, but I felt I needed to get something done, like our budget or cleaning our room. I always felt too tired to attack these tasks. I also needed to send a follow-up email to the caseworker to remind her to take care of Madison's dental concerns. I'd been talking to her about them since before the girls moved in, sending reminders via voicemail, personal conversations, and emails to no avail.

A couple of days later

I was having a hard time tracking the girls' stories. I had been typing up the experiences they had shared with me to email the caseworker so she and the judge could decide what was best for the girls. I finally made it through everything in the girls' binders of notes kept by previous foster moms.

We were their eighth foster home. I had to take notes and date them to refer back to in case of changing stories. It also helped me realize I wasn't crazy. Sometimes when I thought a behavior was a phase, I was surprised to look back and realize how long the behavior had gone on or how long I'd been asking a caseworker to take care of an issue. Notes helped me see when something needed to be done, such as calling a supervisor. They helped me not to second-guess myself or feel as guilty when I needed to request that a child move into a new home.

Sometimes caseworkers' stories change and leave me wondering if I misunderstood or exaggerated a point in my head. Then, when I reread my notes, they offer clarity. I don't take notes on everything, but caseworkers' shared thoughts and perceptions based on facts are helpful later in maintaining my sanity.

The next week

Exhausted. I realized that we might have been the girls' ninth foster home. The girls talked about another foster mom who was not on the list I had, but I wasn't sure how she fit into the story. I found out that the girls lived with a pastor of a church for a short time too. So that made us the tenth family.

The following week

The mental shifting of gears was stripping my emotional transmission. The girls switched quickly from appropriately happy interactions to uncomfortably assertive affection to violent reactions.

Madison wanted to hold my hand *a lot,* kiss both my cheeks, and stop me to say goodbye every time I stepped outside. It was so suffocating and uncomfortable. I would have to talk to her about it again. Setting boundaries with children who need to receive and express affection after experiencing rejection from their parents wasn't something I had thought about before fostering.

The girls were endearing as they snuggled up close while we watched a movie and ate popcorn. Those times were heartwarming. I enjoyed those moments because I knew the predictable hours of disruptive talking, hollering, and temper tantrums were still real. I knew this would level out, and we would come to a new normal that met in the middle between the girls' place of seeming chaos and our family life.

Lord, I need you to be my strength in this process.

The next day

I went to play therapy with Ava. We were going to start going every other week. I didn't know how I felt about it. It was uncomfortable. I couldn't be myself because everything I was doing and saying was being observed and evaluated.

It surprised me when the counselor asked Ava who I was, and she said, "Robin."

Ava called me Mom right away after Madison asked if she could call us Mom and Dad within the first hour they moved in. I was used to the girls referring to their birth mom as their "real mom," and it seemed natural and comfortable. When the counselor referred to me as Miss Robin after Ava's introduction, it made me feel isolated and separated from Ava, and while I tried to take it in stride, it hurt my feelings.

Summertime

One gorgeous, sunny day, we went swimming at the lake, and all the girls got along really well. When we got home, Jerry grilled hamburgers, and we watched a movie together as a family. It felt as though all was right in our world at that moment.

A couple of days later

It was a beautiful day for a hike. The kids and I went on a lot of local day hikes as I trained for a weeklong hiking and camping adventure with a friend at the end of the month. We headed an hour out of town. Ezra, Christianna, Madison and I went on a rigorous ten-mile hike. When I got winded, I stopped to take pictures of the breathtaking views. The kids ran up ahead and then looped back to me.

None of the kids complained, and Madison had an endless supply of energy. She became competitive about being the first on the trail. I had to talk to her repeatedly when she raced around me and then stopped suddenly to look at something on the ground. I kept tripping over her on the narrow path as we descended steep hills and my heavy backpack pushed me forward. Overall, the day was very fun, sprinkled with moments of exhilaration and bits of frustration with Madison. We saw expansive views that outshone some of the images I've seen in outdoor hiking magazines!

Two days later

It was okay that life was full and messy. Wherever I was, I needed to live deeply. Don't worry about the rest. Focus on who I am with and what I am doing.

The next month

Pressure had been silently building within me with all of the kids and responsibilities. We were all back to school, and I had a challenging class that year. I had blatant defiance during the day, sandwiched between tantrums and outbursts at home before and after school.

Even though we had told the caseworker we were open to adopting the girls if that became an option, I was beginning to question whether we should.

The next week

I had no break from challenging behaviors. Teaching an impulsive class of six-year-olds was a test of my patience. Incidents came at me all day like balls from a pitching machine that had gone out of control. I couldn't keep up this frenetic pace. I hit some strikes and missed the balls that were just out of reach or came in behind my back. I had to learn to bat social issues while continuing to teach all day long.

God, I need supernatural wisdom, grace, joy, and peace. Thank you that you can do immeasurably more than I can think or imagine (Eph. 3:20). My life feels as though I'm engaged in a full-contact sport. I need to be physically and mentally quick. Show me how to focus on essential things with confidence today. I don't want to give you or the important people in my life scraps of time or leftover energy.

The following day

Earlier in the week Ava had lashed out in anger several times between episodes of cuddliness and declarations of "I love you, Mommy!" After a challenging day of naughtiness in my first-grade classroom, I was in a state of ragged numbness when I picked up the girls from daycare.

As I came out of the building, I looked up and saw a breathtaking sunset spread out before me. A ray of brilliant yellowy-orange shot down through the middle of the sky like a spotlight. As I walked to the car with Ava's warm little hand in mine, I drank in the beauty with my eyes and peace washed over me. The verse I had read during my morning devotions replayed in my mind: "May the God of hope fill you with all joy and peace as you trust in him, so that you may overflow with hope by the power of the Holy Spirit" (Rom. 15:13).

6

Who Are Foster Kids and What Are Some of Their Thoughts?

"Be strong and courageous. Do not be afraid; do not be discouraged, for the LORD your God will be with you wherever you go." Joshua 1:9

I have been amazed over and over by how resilient the human spirit is. I am humbled by God's grace when a child's innocence is maintained despite horrendous experiences.

While some of the following foster children's comments are disturbing and heartbreaking, they give me the conviction that although I might not know how to parent every child and their issues,

I can provide a safe place for children to sleep. I can love them and let them know they are not alone. A caring adult can make a profound difference in the life of a child by just being there to offer a safe home. Children do not need perfect parents. They need to know they are loved and discover what it feels like to be safe so they can just be kids.

Children's Voices: Comments Made by Foster Children

A five-year-old boy said, "I miss my mom. I like you guys taking care of me because it's scary being on my own."

A ten-year-old girl asked vehemently, "How come you won't let me go back to my mom?"

Every foster child in our home asks, "Can I play your piano?"

A seven-year-old girl studied the floor. "In my last foster home, they wouldn't let me sit on the furniture. I had to sit on the floor because I have lice."

A thirteen-year-old girl looked out the car window. "I need some time before I talk to my parents. If we see them in the store, I'd rather not say hi. I'm so glad I was able to get away from them. I hope I get to go stay with one of my aunts, but I'm relieved to be here, away from my parents."

A nine-year-old girl hollered as she ran to her room, "You're not my mom! But Ezra is my brother!" Ezra, was five months old at the time and she loved to snuggle him.

An eleven-year-old girl had a gym bag on the floor filled with her new Christmas toys. When she pooped in the bag, I asked if she pooped on the floor at her house. She confidently replied, "Yes. My dogs and my brother poop on the floor too. Our toilet doesn't work. Sometimes we poop in the trash can."

Every child asks, "Can I play outside?"

A nine-year-old girl leaned against me and said, "I love you."

When a ten-year-old foster daughter was taking a bath, I opened the door to put clean clothes on the counter. She proudly pointed at her lap and said, "Look! I have hair down there. My mom's boyfriend says he likes it."

"How did he see it?" I asked.

"I sleep in between him and my mom," she informed me.

After leaving our home, a five-year-old girl we saw at a school event said, "I wish we could be with you again."

Before getting ready for bed in my son's room, a three-year-old boy bravely asserted, "Where should I change? He gonna look?"

Most kids ask, "Can I help cook?"

Every foster child asks, "Where is the cat?"

A seven-year-old girl helped me mix cookie dough. "My mom's boyfriend used to tie my mom up with zip ties and hit her. She didn't have clothes on."

A ten-year-old foster daughter walked alongside me down the street and asked, "Will you adopt us?"

A six-year-old boy looked up at me expectantly, "What's your favorite kidable movie?"

Every elementary-aged foster child asks, "Can we go to the playground?"

"My mom's boyfriend used to make me drink beer before school, and he put a shaky thing on me down there," a seven-year-old girl remembered. "It hurt. He would go into my little sister's room and she would holler and cry, but I don't know what he did to her."

A six-year-old talked about making dinner for herself and her little brother. "I can cook. I used to cook dinner when my mom was gone a long time. I always made toast."

"I'm embarrassed," a shy eight-year-old girl confessed as we drove up to her school, "'cause you're all white."

"I'm not ready for a foster family yet. Please just take me back to the shelter. I need a cigarette or some weed! I love you guys, but I just can't live with you." This sixteen-year-old foster daughter's plea became her mantra until we agreed to ask her caseworker to find her a placement in a treatment facility.

Before returning to his parents' care in a tiny village across the state, a ten-year-old boy asked, "Can I see you again after I go home?"

A four-year-old girl looked up as me as I tied her shoes. "I love you."

The other day, I chatted on the phone with our grown daughter we adopted through foster care, and she said, "My life is better because you guys adopted me."

As I reread these slivers of conversations, my heart aches and I long for God's protection over these innocent children and many others with stories like these. "He will cover you with his feathers, and under his wings you will find refuge; his faithfulness will be your shield and rampart" (Ps. 91:4).

Notes from My Journal: The Story Continues

One sad day

The girls had dried tear tracks down their faces when they came home from visiting their mom. As Madison came into the house, she began recounting their visit.

"My mom said, 'Is this what you want to do to me and my

girls?' And the caseworker said, 'We're not going to talk about this in front of the girls.'"

"What were they talking about?" I asked.

"They're going to court tomorrow, and they're going to have us adopted to someone. My mom just needs to find a job and get a car," she objected, as if that was the only reason she and her little sister were still living with us.

"Children are not taken away from their parents because they don't have work," I said as I continued to load the washing machine. "It's a mom's job to keep her children safe. That's my job with all of you. You haven't always been safe with your mom." I closed the washer and turned to look her in the eye. "A judge doesn't want to take children away from their parents, but if parents aren't keeping their children safe, the judge has to find a safe family for the kids. You can pray that the judge will make the right decision. God knows what is best for you and Ava. You can pray for your mom. God knows what is best for her too."

Madison and I prayed together, and her prayer was so heartfelt. She even prayed for the judge. Madison always thanked God for the people he brought into her and Ava's lives and his plan for them. Her depth and thoughtfulness astounded me.

Looking back

In the first couple of weeks after moving in, Madison asked a lot of questions about adoption and being adopted in general. She presented many scenarios beginning with "If you adopted us would . . . or could . . ." I never brought up adoption, but I answered Madison's questions since adoption was so heavy on her mind. I told her no one knew what was going to happen, but everyone wanted to make sure she was safe.

I got the impression that while Madison would have loved to be with her mom, she wanted to be a part of a stable family just as much, even if it meant being adopted, which was a frightening thought to her.

Madison loved her mom as she was designed to. Babies and children inherently attach to their parents who are meant to protect and nurture them as they grow to become independent one day.

One of the Ten Commandments says, "Honor your father and your mother, so that you may live long in the land the LORD your God is giving you" (Ex. 20:12). Later, this truth is reiterated in the New Testament: "Children, obey your parents in the Lord, for this is right. 'Honor your father and mother'—which is the first commandment with a promise—'so that it may go well with you and that you may enjoy long life on the earth.' Fathers, do not exasperate your children; instead, bring them up in the training and instruction of the Lord" (Eph. 6:1–4).

Reflection

Generally, I do not question or think about why things are the way they are. That seems to be true of foster children too. I've found that foster children do not have the same assumptions about life as I do because they have had different experiences growing up.

Aside from two high school girls, the oldest foster child who came into our care was ten years old. Here are some of the assumptions about ordinary life our foster children have communicated.

- It is their job to take care of their mom.
- When parents leave for extended times or overnight, you take care of yourself and your siblings.
- When you sleep in between your mom and her boyfriend, he touches you everywhere and wants you to touch him.
- You don't have to be careful with things. They don't last, and someone will always give you another one.
- Cops are scary and take away the people you love.
- No matter where you go, bad men always find you and your mom. When your mom tells you to hide from men. Cops, landlords, and boyfriends can all get angry and scary.

Maybe because these assumptions are learned, children do not recognize when their parents are doing something wrong. Children might not understand that the things happening to them are not okay because a parent has allowed people in their life to do things to them that no child should ever experience. Children might not know it is abuse.

Most often, despite these realities for many children, the attachment they have to their parents is still strong. Somehow the bond is not broken even when the biological parent inflicts injury through the trauma of abuse and neglect. Maybe the fear somehow adheres them together in a primal instinct to survive together after all they have endured. Children often think their reality is the way life is for everyone.

A few days later

Little Ava warmed my heart as she danced and sang her prayers. She prayed for everyone in our house, including our pets. Our cat, dog, and guinea pigs were well prayed for by name each day. She loved to give hugs and crawl into my lap for snuggles and stories.

Madison was thoughtful and articulate. She learned to figure out life by watching those around her and putting clues together. Some nights I wished I was recording her prayers. They were so uniquely specific. Madison was also very assertive about asking for what she wanted or needed.

She liked to go to piano lessons with the other kids and play with the toys there. When she asked if she could play the piano too, I said, "Next year when school starts again, you can choose an instrument to play. School's out in six weeks, and we don't take piano lessons in the summer." *Honestly, I can't handle any more time or money obligations. I'm stretched to the max.*

Madison replied, "But what if I'm not here next year?"

"We have adventures and trips this summer!" I replied. "We're all going to have a lot of fun!"

The next month

The play therapist said that the girls were deeply affected by their trauma. I asked what that meant, and she explained that Ava only bonds superficially, partly due to having so many "parents" in a relatively short time. I don't understand yet. I've just been amazed at their resiliency.

The therapist first met Ava when she was two. After being in foster care for a year and a half, the girls went back to their mom for a few months before they were removed again. The counselor wanted to help Ava make a book of the people she stayed with so she could remember them as she got older.

The therapist was happy to hear that Ava was not harming herself anymore. I didn't know that she used to hurt herself. Apparently, Ava used to scratch herself until she bled at times. The therapist said she would like to be in better communication with the caseworker so we could work together and share information as a team to help the girls progress.

Later that week

Madison was crying when she came into the kitchen, where I was preparing dinner. She asked to talk to me alone. Madison shared that her mom had to go to court again the next day.

After talking to her counselor, Madison was afraid that she wouldn't be able to see her mom again until she was fifteen or sixteen. I explained to her that the caseworker and judge were trying to make the best decision for her and Ava. They gave birth parents lots of chances. Everyone wanted to make sure she would be safe.

I explained, "Sometimes bad things happen, and it's not the parent's fault, but it is the parent's job to get away from dangerous situations so their children can be safe. The judge let you go back to your mom once, and you got hurt again. You have lived with a lot of families. Was that hard?"

"Yes," she replied.

"It is best for kids to have a family they can stay with who can love them and help them to grow up into healthy adults. Does that make sense?"

"Yes," Madison responded.

"God has a special plan for you, Madison, and he will be with you if you go back to live with your mom or if you are adopted. He will always be with you."

I prayed that the girls and their birth mom would have peace and feel God's love. I also prayed that facts would be shared in court without exaggeration and the judge would know without wavering what the right decision was for the girls.

Madison, brave as can be, prayed through her tears "that all the adults would know what the best decision is to make and that anyone that has back pain would be healed. And help the judge not to be afraid of making the wrong decision. God, fill our house and yard with angels and love, that no harm would come to us. Thank you for all the people you have brought into our lives and all the people that you haven't. And help us not to have bad dreams."

In tears, I agreed, "Amen."

The caseworker said their mom was still working toward getting the girls back. After this was clarified, the girls had a phone call or two with their mom, and then we found out she was moving out of the area. After the girls said goodbye, we didn't hear from their mom or the caseworker for an extended time. Since it was the end of the school year, we had a lot of fun things planned, and no one seemed to notice how fast time passed.

Summertime

The girls did well when their mom became unreachable for a few months. We made fun memories, and the drama mellowed out. Temper tantrums became fewer and shorter, and the girls got along better. Madison was kinder to all the kids. I rarely heard her say mean things to Ava to make her cry on purpose. Over the course of a couple of months, Ava's reactions improved too. When I said no to Ava, she went from having tantrums, to crying or arguing for a couple of minutes, to finally saying, "Okay, Mommy. Can I watch a movie after dinner then?" without crying! It felt like a miracle!

The kids played outside every day. We had a fun summer swimming and kayaking at local lakes and playing at the park. Summer camp and Vacation Bible School added to the excitement too.

For the longest time, the girls didn't ask about their mom. We were having fun being a family. The girls continued to go to play therapy each week, and one day the therapist mentioned that Madison was worried about her mom.

During the school year, when Madison had regular visits with her mom twice a week, she came home happy. But by evening time, she would come to me crying. She would perseverate on something her mom said or how she thought her mom acted until Madison was sure something terrible was going to happen. Because of this, I avoided bringing up her mom, but I was open to talking about her. If Madison or Ava talked about their mom, I asked questions about the memories and stories they shared.

After the therapist mentioned that Madison was worried about her mom but she hadn't mentioned it to me, I realized I needed to talk to her. I didn't want her to think that she couldn't talk about her mom.

I pulled her aside and said, "If you ever want to talk about your mom, you can talk to me about her. I like to hear the stories you share, and if you have questions, I can try to answer them. I know sometimes you worry, so I don't bring her up because I don't want to cause you to worry. It's not because I don't want you to talk about her."

"Okay," she replied, and after that, she asked a couple of times if I had heard from the caseworker, saying, "I wonder when we're going to talk to my mom again." I answered honestly that I hadn't heard back from the caseworker and didn't know when the next telephone visit with her mom would happen.

I called the caseworker once in a while to see what was going on, but she didn't answer the phone or return phone calls often. When I did get hold of the caseworker, I found out their mom had disappeared for a while. Their mom spent time between different communities, and the caseworker had a hard time reaching her when their mom didn't return calls and then lost her phone.

The next month

The girls spoke to their mom on the phone again for the first time in a long time. She even came to town for a visit. Everything seemed to take a negative turn. Ava was angry and became aggressive—scratching, kicking, and spitting. Madison became emotional and fearful. It had been seven months since they moved in.

One day, Ava was mad at the world in general as she was getting in the car for daycare. She hit Madison and yelled vehemently, "I'm going to call the cops on you!" Madison began hollering back, and they both started crying.

"The cops are going to come and take us away! You're going to call the cops on us!" Madison hollered.

"Stop! No one is calling the cops! We're not saying that! The two of you will always be sisters, and you need to learn to be nice to each other," I said firmly but exasperatedly. "Ava, are you really going to call the cops on Madison?"

"No," she spat out.

"Then don't say you are. Cops keep us safe when people are trying to hurt us, but it's my job as the mom to help you learn to be nice to each other. When Ava said she'd call the cops, you both went crazy with fear and anger. Madison, did you feel how that felt when Ava said she was going to call the cops?"

"Yes," she replied grudgingly.

"Are you planning on calling the cops on Ava?"

"No."

"We're *not* going to say we're calling the cops when it's not true and it makes everyone feel like *that* just felt. We're not doing that to each other. If you get mad or frustrated with each other, you are going to learn to talk about it."

Ava erupted, "I want to go live with my mom! How come she only takes care of my brother? She loves me!" The last couple of times the girls talked to their mom, she told them she was going to see their brother.

"She does love you," I sighed.

"How come she doesn't come to see us?" Ava asked.

"How come she didn't get on the plane?" Madison's heart broke. (Since communities in Alaska can be remote, the state provides airfare for visits when needed).

"I don't know," I replied truthfully.

I turned on some calming music as we drove in silence. Sometimes, I just don't know what to say, and that is part of the fostering experience too.

How Do I Prepare for the Unexpected, Including an Investigation?

*"I pray that out of his glorious riches he may strengthen you
with power through his Spirit in your inner being."* Ephesians 3:16

T his was the big day! I was running late to meet up with my friend
to begin our epic adventure. I was nervous about attempting my
first "hike-through" camping trip. My blood pressure rose as I searched
for my passport. *Where did I put it? I should have left ten minutes ago!*
We planned to camp in Canada that night and arrive at the trailhead
the next day after more driving. Jerry helped me look for the elusive
passport.

Suddenly, there was a knock on the door. Three workers from
Child Services stood before me. "We're here to investigate the safety of
the children," one said.

My heart stopped.

"Come in," I said as my mind raced. *Who reported us to Child
Services? What did they say we did?* I looked at Jerry for support. The
three investigators sat down in the living room.

"How do you handle discipline in your home?" the first woman asked as she looked sternly to Jerry and then to me.

"We tell children what we expect before there is a problem. When Ava hurts someone, she sits in time-out at the table. We talk to the kids when they do or say something inappropriate," I answered honestly as my heart raced.

"You don't ever spank your children?"

"We spanked our own children when they were small and it was a matter of their safety. I can't remember when we spanked one of our kids last." I nervously shifted in my chair as I raked my memory. "We have probably spanked each of our kids three or four times in their lifetime." Then I shared two examples of when we had spanked Ezra.

When our son was three and a half, he would hide from us and then silently watch us from his hiding spot as our worry escalated. We had already talked to him a couple of times about how this scared Mommy and Daddy, and it was our job to keep him safe and he had to help us.

One evening after I tucked him in for the night, I walked by his room and saw that his bed was empty. I called for him and checked the two spots he had hidden in previously. Then I called for him in the yard. I knocked on doors up and down the street, asking neighbors if they had seen him. I was getting frantic. Twilight was quickly turning to night as I walked down the street. Then I saw him, standing in the corner of the park with his back to a stop sign at the intersection, quietly watching me and my husband call for him! Relief and anger washed over me. I spanked him—two swats with my hand on his bottom through his pj's and pull-up diaper. He did not hide from us after that.

When Ezra was five, we lived in a village in Alaska with no cars. Everyone walked. One evening he refused to walk home from the town hall with me (the equivalent of a block and a half). It was twenty degrees below zeo and the wind was blowing hard. These were typical conditions during winter where we lived. About half a block from the town hall, he stopped and refused to move. There was about a foot of loose snow on the ground that evening, and I was carrying two-year-old, Christianna, and I needed him to walk! I could not talk him into walking, and it was cold! It was a matter of safety. I gave him one spank on the bottom through his snowsuit, and he walked home.

"We have not spanked our foster girls," I asserted. I took a deep breath to share a recent event.

"My mom visited recently, and she stayed home with the girls when I went to the store one day. All our girls love her, and I wasn't worried about leaving them. While I was gone, Ava had a royal meltdown about something that seemed fairly insignificant. She let out an ear-splitting cry that was an inappropriate response to whatever she wanted or didn't want to do. She began hitting from under the kitchen table and refused to come out. My mom spanked her, one swift swat on the bottom."

I didn't think to tell my mom she wasn't allowed to spank a foster child. Ava's colossal tantrums were becoming less and less common, and she loved doing anything with my mom. I wasn't even gone that long.

Honestly, through all the caseworkers' questioning, I did a lot of crying. The crazy thing was that the previous day, I had been talking to a friend on the phone who said, "You are the best mom I know. You're so good with your kids. You're so patient. And Jerry is so good with the kids too."

The workers then told us that two of them needed to interview our biological children separately.

"We are doing foster care because we want to provide a safe home for kids," I retorted as my anger and tears flowed. "It is insulting and feels invasive that you want to interview our children individually."

"It's our job to investigate any concerns. You wouldn't want us to ignore reports, because sometimes they are valid. That's how we protect children," one of the lead investigators explained earnestly.

I understood that on a logical level, but I was still devastated that someone could think that we would intentionally cause harm to a child. *I'm a teacher. I was voted "Teacher of the Year" by all the staff at my school one year! And Jerry is so good with the kids. He plays with them all the time.*

One worker stayed with my husband and me to make sure we didn't coach our kids about what they were supposed to say while the other two went and talked to our children in the girls' bedroom. Later, our kids told us they were asked if their parents fight. They were also asked, "How do your parents get you to do things when you don't listen to them?" Then they were asked how Ava goes to bed at night.

After talking to our children one at a time, the workers returned to the living room and told us sternly that we were not allowed to spank foster children or allow them to see us spank our biological children because they have experienced physical trauma and it could trigger painful memories. The caseworkers then explained that if we left them with someone else, we were still responsible for whatever happened to them. And we were not allowed to withhold food for any reason.

"We don't withhold food from our children!" I straightened in my chair indignantly.

The worker replied, "The kids said that if they don't clean their room, they don't get dessert. Withholding food when others are eating is a form of punishment. And you cannot force children to eat anything by saving it until they eat it."

I leaned forward earnestly. "The girls are good eaters. We've never made them eat anything. If they are full, we don't make them eat any more. They just can't have seconds of something if they say they are too full to eat what's already on their plate, but that has never been an issue. As an incentive to clean up, I tell everyone that when our rooms are clean, we can have dessert. We don't have dessert very often, but Madison and Ava ask for it every day. Sometimes, we use dessert as an incentive to get everyone's room clean. If the kids get their rooms clean, they can have dessert any time before they brush their teeth for bed. If they don't clean their room, they don't get dessert."

"If one person in your family has dessert, everyone has to be offered dessert. You cannot use food to control children," the caseworker reprimanded. "And the plant above your TV on top of the kitchen cupboards is a poisonous plant. That is in violation."

A philodendron is one of the most common houseplants I've noticed in homes. My mom always had one in our home growing up. It is a plant with heart-shaped leaves, often seen wrapping around the walls of a classroom or across shelves in a children's library. After the workers left, I looked it up online. I read that philodendrons are poisonous when they are consumed by young children or pets.

"We'll go to the daycare now and interview the girls," one of the workers said as they all stood.

Feeling lost and in desperate need of closure, I stood too. "I was on my way out of town when you stopped in. My friend and I trained for two months for a trek over the Chilkoot Trail, and we have reservations for a cabin and a train ride back. We're supposed to be in Canada tonight." I looked from one of the lead caseworkers to the other.

"You can go ahead and go. We'll let you know what comes of our investigation in a day or two," one worker said cheerfully.

"I'll have spotty phone service through Canada tonight and tomorrow, and then I'll be hiking and have no access to phone service for a week."

"You can find out when you get back. Jerry, if we have further questions, we'll be back after we talk to the girls. We don't want to keep you. Have fun!" one of the workers smiled.

Now in addition to carrying my bear spray and figuring out the best way to cross running creeks and rivers as we climb over the mountain, I'll have to try not to worry about being investigated! I thought exasperatedly. Adrenaline still running high, I *told myself, it is going to be what it is going to be. Lord, I trust you. Help me not to worry about all our children.*

I prayed that prayer a few times during our trek through beauty that declared God's sovereignty all around me. Each time after I

prayed, I felt God's peace that was beyond understanding wash over me. I knew to my very core that, even there, he saw me and he loved me. And I trusted him.

We received a letter about a week later stating that we were found not guilty of inflicting physical and emotional harm on the children. However, due to violations, we needed to take a remedial class on appropriate ways to get children to comply.

As requested, we wrote a statement:

We will notify anyone we leave the children with that no corporal punishment is allowed. We acknowledge that their care is our responsibility as adults, and that it is our responsibility to defuse situations when a child's behavior escalates.

The paperwork on food in the training packet stated simply that we could not withhold food from children as a punishment. Honestly, I do not believe that was what we were doing, but we completed the class. And, to the girls' chagrin, we went back to having fewer desserts the way we did before they moved in because we could not offer dessert as an incentive. I also removed the offending plant from the house.

This has been the hardest part of the book to write so far. Honestly, during the investigation, Jerry added to the conversation too. I was too emotional then to remember how he responded, and I am the assertive one between the two of us, so this is my reflection. There the ugly, honest truth is. The investigation was a horrifying experience, but we survived it. Honestly, we thought about quitting foster care. It was that terrifying to me. I'm used to always trying to do what is right, and the thought that someone would think I have evil intentions shook me.

We decided to continue to foster because our girls had been through so much already, and I didn't want them to have to move again.

Since this experience, I make myself available to listen to supervised visits over the phone between the caseworker, parents, and children. This way, if children say things that could be misinterpreted, I can address them right away.

I was told in foster care classes that you *will* have an investigation at some point if you foster long enough. I wasn't ready. Maybe by hearing about this humbling experience, you will be less shocked when it happens to you, and you will handle it with less fear and fewer tears.

One of the workers I met at the investigation has become an ally as she has investigated the safety of children in my classroom. Since the investigation, she has called to place foster children in our home.

What she told me that traumatic day of the investigation was true. It is their job to investigate concerns about children's safety, and sometimes concerns in foster homes are valid. That's how they protect children. If some of our foster children went on to another foster home and they were being abused, I would want it investigated.

8

How Do I
Find Support?

"Encourage one another and build each other up."

1 Thessalonians 5:11a

You shouldn't foster alone. If you want to parent well, without imploding, use the resources you have around you. We all need support!

A child's recovery and growth after surviving trauma is not a foster parent's responsibility alone. We need to guard our minds

and hearts against the natural tendency to mentally take on the sole responsibility of fostering children. Caseworkers, therapists, teachers, and other advocates, including friends and family members, all contribute to the development of a child.

Ultimately, God knows each child's needs and reactions better than we ever will, and we must trust that he will be with each child even if there comes a time when we are no longer a daily part of their life. Sometimes we don't get to see how far a child will move beyond their trauma, but we can trust God to continue his work in their life. As a friend said in our fostering support group last week, "Love is never wasted."

Each foster parent is a part of a child's life for a reason. We parent the best we can, and sometimes we get to witness a child's growth in our home. As they move outside of our sight, we must trust that God will go with them. Our sphere of influence and protection may be just as strong if we commit to surrounding them in prayer.

You will need support as a foster parent, and the support that you reach for will often be your friends. Most of us have heard it is important to choose friends wisely. In surviving foster care, this is vital. If you can, establish healthy relationships before you are in a time of crisis. Wherever you are in life, start now.

When you step out of your comfort zone and initiate friendships, others are grateful. Here are some ways I stepped out of my comfort zone. I joined a local foster support group on Facebook, and my husband and I volunteered to lead a group study using a book like this one, written by a foster parent. At our group study, we discussed the stories in the book and any issues and concerns that arose as they related to the kids in our homes, and we prayed for each other. Two families who were curious about foster care joined our group and became foster families after our study.

As we shared concerns and complications in our schedules, people in the group volunteered to meet needs—everything from helping a single mom who wanted a healthy male role model for her son to finding healthy friends for our kids with attentive parents.

Outside this group, my husband began including a boy from a foster family on fishing trips with our kids. He didn't have a dad at home. I met up with another single foster mom to play at the park so our shy kids had a chance to become friends while we moms shared resources we discovered.

Who knew Child Services in our state had a yearly activity stipend that will pay $150 toward things like swim lessons, piano lessons, or a bike? They even have a separate camp stipend for foster kids! Visiting with other moms is how I discovered that every foster child five and under automatically qualifies for the federal Special Supplemental Nutrition Program for Women, Infants, and Children (WIC), which includes lots of free groceries. These visits were also where I exchanged phone numbers with moms who volunteered to pick things up for our kids across town and take our foster kids for sleepovers to give us a break. One mom picked up school lunches every day and left them by our door the week I was sick and we were in quarantine as I waited for COVID-19 test results.

When we went camping with another foster family, a young, single foster mom asked if she could join us. It pays to be assertive. While my husband helped her boys learn to fish and use slingshots, she figured out the details of camping and shared her heart with the other moms. It was a great break, and we all had a lot of fun!

Seek out and develop relationships with the people who energize you, inspire you, and feed your soul. Sometimes we find people we admire, but somehow, we come away feeling guilty about not doing as much as they are doing. These are not the people you should seek out.

Who would you like to become more like? Who would you like to learn from? If it isn't someone you already know well, be brave and ask them if they would like to meet for coffee sometime this week. You could meet with your kids at the park, sit together at an event, or go for a walk. Set a date. If you don't act now, you will blink and realize a year or two has gone by and you are still missing out on an inspiring friendship.

There is nothing as helpful as connecting with other foster parents who understand the contradictions of the waiting and the urgencies of fostering. There is nothing worse than being undermined by well-meaning friends who respond to your venting by saying, "I could never foster. Why do you put up with that? Do you think that's the best thing for you right now?"

Get contact information for people you connect with at foster classes. You never know when you will need to compare experiences and ask specific advice about caseworkers, kids, and the whole process. Then, be intentional about developing a relationship with at least one foster parent in whom you can confide. Trust me. You will need this relationship.

I have always been in awe of foster moms who maintain three or more foster kids in addition to their birth children. Recently, we ended up increasing the number of foster children in our home from two to three so a sibling who was by herself could join her sisters who were in our care. Somehow, when I'm the one doing the best I can with a houseful, I don't feel inspiring. I'm thankful God sees me where I am and sends help when I need it most.

When I visit with moms at foster care support meetings, their stories give me perspective, and I am thankful I don't have their challenges. These parents are in the trenches. They are holding the kids who are up crying in the middle of the night, doing mountains of laundry when they are exhausted, following through with consequences to teach a child to respect others when it would be easier to let it go. They are logging conversations with caseworkers and following up on documented issues to make sure children's needs are met. These parents admit at times, "I don't know how we do it." They are full-on superheroes in my mind! They are doing it amid the excitement of an ever-evolving family. Their stories make me thankful for the big kids I have at home who help make dinner and the endearing foster children I currently have who are so respectful.

If you don't know how to connect with other foster parents, start by looking online. There is likely a Facebook group for foster parents in your area. In these groups, parents can ask questions about caseworkers, how the foster system in their area works, and even how to find homes that have space available for children who need a new home.

We all need objective people in our lives, and I make a point of seeking advice from seasoned Christians ahead of me in parenting even when they have not been foster parents. It helps to have friends who can be objective and are willing to tell you the truth in difficult times.

When you begin to get overwhelmed, it can be natural to isolate yourself. Sometimes you may feel grumpy or sad, and you won't feel like being around anyone. Be careful how long you let yourself stay in this state, or it can sabotage your whole life. Sometimes a break is exactly what you need to renew your energy.

What refreshes you? Is it nature? Music? Exercise? Certain things naturally refresh us, such as exercise, smiling, and laughter. These actions release endorphins in our brains that can lighten a sour mood. Notice these are *actions*—things you need to *do* to make yourself feel better. Take action before you sink into a pit of ugly-colored feelings. It is easier to rebound from blue feelings before they swirl into gray or black.

A few times, I found myself immersed in black feelings, and I wondered how I got there without realizing I was slipping into the pit. At those times, pressure and responsibilities gradually built up until I suddenly jerked awake to being strangled! In times of clarity, when I felt like I was being overtaken by my schedule, I looked at specific details in my life. I thought, I *can handle that child's difficult behavior and this activity, and that thing I need to do isn't hard; I just need to do it.* Then I realized, *Yes, I can do all those things and the other twenty-seven things I am doing and do them well, but not all at the same time!*

I grew up hearing, "Ask and it will be given to you" (Matt. 7:7a). One week I had so much to do at school. I was going to take down a bulletin board and put up a new one, but I stopped and prayed, *Lord would you send someone to do this for me today?* I worked on preparing individual student assignments instead.

That afternoon, someone I had never met randomly stopped by

my room and asked if I needed help with anything. She was subbing for another teacher and had some spare time. Someone in the office had suggested I might need help. I am so thankful for the generosity of the people God inspires to look out for me. I was reminded of the verse "My help comes from the LORD" (Ps. 121:2a).

Subs can be hard to get in our school district. When I was feeling sick at school one day, I texted a sub during recess to ask if she could take my class the next day. "I can come over now," she texted back. She showed up in my classroom fifteen minutes later and changed an appointment so she could sub for me the following day too. I told her I hadn't typed up sub plans, and she said, "Just tell me what you had in mind."

After a ten-minute conversation with her about my classroom schedule, she said, "Go home and rest. I can take care of your class." I got to go home to a quiet house and sleep before my kids came home from school. I was so thankful. God does send unexpected help, and I need to recognize these little gifts of favor.

It's often hard to decide how to simplify life. Most of us need to open up our schedule enough to allow room to breathe. If I can't function well in my role, then it will affect everyone else.

I love living life together as a family, but I often find myself involved in everyone's activities as Taxi-Mom. I am learning to let go a little bit and allow my husband to take the kids to a school family night while I stay home on occasion. We have had conversations about everyone staying home a given time and going to the next school event as a family. Let go of the pressure to attend every school, church, or extracurricular activity. My mom told me, "Sometimes you need to lower your expectations."

Some ways we have improved our time together is by working together as a family. We all like to have big breakfasts on the weekends, but I don't always have time before church to get it all on the table and get us out the door on time. For one of our favorite meals, Ezra makes homemade berry sauce while I make blueberry pancakes, and one of the girls sets the table. Afterward, my husband or Shariah, supervises the cleanup while I get ready for church.

We also limit the number of activities we participate in. The kids can choose two sport seasons a year so I don't feel like I have to live in the car, driving them back and forth. To meet this guideline, Ezra went from being on the year-round city swim team to the school swim team, which runs only a couple of months a year. Since school sports are on campus after school, this eliminated the need to pick him up and then drop him off elsewhere.

Although limiting his swim season was initially a hard decision to make, ultimately Ezra didn't get tired of going to practices anymore, and we all looked forward to his meets during his short season. I also noticed that Ezra's mood improved when his schedule wasn't as busy.

When our kids were in too many activities, we often ran out of time for chores. By the time they crammed in homework, it was late. We then got up and did the whole thing again! Our house got messier and messier. Limiting activities provided downtime for the kids to be kids. Instead of bouncing back and forth between school and sports, the kids were able to play card games, ride bikes, make origami, jump on the trampoline, and develop a love for going to the library.

I want to model healthy living choices for our children. Others will not always clean up after them in life. Our children are expected to clean their rooms, put their own things away around the house, and help with dishes. If they don't keep their rooms clean all week, they do not get paid on Saturday. If they don't finish dishes on their day, no worries. They get to do dishes until the kitchen is completely cleaned. If that is after breakfast the next day, then whoever had dishes that next morning gets the meal off. If they don't finish the dishes until the next night, then whoever had dishes that day gets a free day!

We make adjustments to the dish days only if there is a change in schedules. Otherwise, rotating schedules requires too much mental energy, judgment calls on whose day it is, and kids crying because they thought it wasn't their day. No thank you! If someone is sick or it's their birthday, we do let the kids trade. They have always been willing, and on the days when they are reluctant, I ask, "Wouldn't you want a day off for your birthday?" or "She will cover for you when you're sick. Today is your turn."

My mantra is based on Philippians 2:14: "We do everything without complaining or arguing." It makes a difference. Our job as parents is to work ourselves out of a job and prepare kids to eventually be able to take care of themselves as responsible adults.

Look at the friends you already have, seek out friends who will support you on this journey, and think about ways you can simplify your schedule. This could be mutually beneficial to a friend or neighbor if you take turns driving or watching each other's kids. Sometimes your friends can be excellent mentors and role models for your children. You can foster and do it well with a lot of intentiality and help from others.

How to Set Yourself Up for Success

"Finally, brothers and sisters, whatever is true, whatever is noble, whatever is right, whatever is pure, whatever is lovely, whatever is admirable—if anything is excellent or praiseworthy—think about such things." Philippians 4:8

Set Limits for Yourself

Have an age range in mind and think about the behaviors you are comfortable with before having a child move in.

It is better to wait for a good fit for your family than to have a child you aren't comfortable with in your home. Saying no to a placement is way less stressful and guilt-inducing before you meet a child than after you already have the child in your home.

Say no to placements when they are beyond your abilities or home situation.

If you love the idea of a baby but know you don't want to be up at night changing diapers, don't say yes to a baby. If one of your children is strongly opposed to sharing a room, and you don't think he or she would do well sharing with a foster child, don't put a foster child in with them.

Ultimately, as parents, we make the decisions for what we think is best for our families. Talking through the fostering process as a family helps prepare everyone for the adventure, and children can become more open as individual situations unfold.

There is an adrenaline rush associated with getting your first foster child. It is difficult to say no when you are excited to start making a difference. I know two families who made exceptions for children outside of their comfort zone. One of my friends said yes, and after a night of worrying over a very sick child, called Child Services to explain she couldn't do it. "What if the child stops breathing?" she worried. She felt horrible about not being able to take care of the child and thought about not going forward with fostering because of her scare. Know that when children come to live with you, they can be ill, have injuries, or have lice, all of which can be very time intensive on top of helping a child get settled into your home.

There May Be Exceptions

Now that I've encouraged you to set limits, know that we do make exceptions at times. As a family, we pray that God will prepare us for our next foster children and that people will have the courage to see and report children who are not safe.

My husband and I agree that if we get a call for a child who is within the guidelines we agreed on, we can say yes without talking to each other. If a child is outside those parameters and we have peace about it, we call and check in with each other about making an exception. Gender only matters to us because foster children have to share a room with our children.

If You Will Need Daycare, Locate Options Before Children Move In

Daycare is challenging to find for the next day. Get the names of certified providers from the local childcare referral system and find out how much Child Services will pay. The state needs to approve daycare payments before they start. Some daycare providers do not take state payments, and others may charge more than the state allocates. You will have to pay the additional amount. Just like a new parent, look into your options ahead of time. Call and talk to providers, visit the daycare, and ask if they have openings.

Plan How Children Will Get To and From School

By law, foster parents have to get foster children to the same school they attended before they went into foster care to have consistency in their lives. If it's not in the child's best interest to continue at their school, a change is possible. If your child needs to ride the bus, call the district to make arrangements. It may take a couple of days to set up. If there is no bus available, parents have to get students to school themselves or arrange to get them there some other way.

Set Boundaries for Parents, Caseworkers, and Children

Think about whether you are comfortable supervising visits with birth parents or letting birth parents call to talk to their children. Are you comfortable with children in your home having cell phones? Parents do have the ability to track phones. Think about your comfort level with these issues ahead of time so that you will be ready to voice your opinion and set boundaries for your household.

Always Be Friendly and Respectful to Birth Parents and Caseworkers

Birth parents can make life difficult for you and cause their child to be moved to a different home. It was surprising that one parent we worked with for a long time did not seem to make efforts to get her child back, but always did the bare minimum to drag out the process. She was going to resist the system the whole way. Then, at one meeting, she unexpectedly said that if my husband and I were willing to adopt her child, she would sign away her parental rights. We have also had parents thank us for taking care of their children.

Decide What Your Role Will Be with Birth Parents

Some foster parents do not interact with birth parents, and others mentor the birth parents along with the child and invite them to be a part of the child's life over the phone, in public places, or sometimes in their own home.

It is easy to find out about parents by looking them up in public criminal records and on Facebook. If a mom is sweet but has a history of having abusive boyfriends, you probably don't want her to know where you live. Setting boundaries is crucial, including how often or when you are comfortable with a parent calling.

If your foster child has behavior issues or becomes distraught after talking to a parent, this can help guide how often or when you initiate communication outside state-supervised visits. Interactions right before bed can dissolve into unending tears or defiance. By having calls or visits earlier in the day, these reactions can sometimes be avoided. Sometimes I let children know we're going to the park or swimming after the visit so they have something to look forward to.

If a child is upset, I let them know that everything is okay. Sometimes I hold a small child tightly and verbalize for them, "I know you're sad and you miss your mommy." Asking if they want to watch a cartoon episode can be a calming transition back into a family routine.

I am cautious and do not send pictures showing my birth children to my foster children's parents. I get to know the parent from interactions at supervised visits or encounters at meetings. Sometimes parents show up to doctor appointments or school conferences. Parents have a right to come to these events, so I share the times with the caseworker or the birth parents. I have found that they are more likely to call in to a meeting then show up in person.

I initially share with the caseworker that I am not comfortable supervising phone visits between parents and children. Children see their parents at the customary visits supervised by a caseworker. It is easier to loosen household guidelines than to add new rules if children and parents are given unlimited access to each other from the beginning.

Don't Overreact When a Child Shares Something Shocking

When children are comfortable, they will share stories of their abuse. Often it is stated as a random fact while you are making dinner or doing something together. If you react in anger or shock, a child will stop sharing. I learned the hard way not to overreact when a foster child told me everyone had to hide during an unsupervised visit. I exclaimed a little too loudly, "He had a knife?" Our usually talkative foster daughter wouldn't tell me any more details, and she said, "I wasn't scared."

Now I usually respond with a calm "That must have been scary" or "Was anyone else there with you?" or "What did you do?" Children will usually fill in more facts. Make sure you email the information to the child's social worker and CC the worker's supervisor and the child's GAL so they can add the incident to their files. Then you will have proof that you sent it. As a mandatory reporter, you may need to call the police or, if it is after hours, the on-call number at Child Services.

Plan How You Will React When a Foster Child Shares Something Shocking in Front of Your Children

A calm voice and a simple response seem to cause less of a reaction all the way around. You could say something like, "That sounds like it was painful/scary/hurtful. If you want to tell me about it, we can go to your room to talk." Otherwise, you could calmly ask the other child or children to go clean their room, work on their homework in a different room, or play outside so you can talk.

Sometimes Secrets Need to Be Shared

Tell your kids that if a foster child shares something scary or something bad that happened, they need to tell you. It's your job as the parent to keep all your kids safe, and it is their job to help you keep everyone safe.

Truths from the Trenches

"Sleep can be spiritual." I thought this remark by my cross-country coach in college was odd at the time. I had worked up the courage to tell him I was too tired to go to Bible study that night. I felt so guilty. Now, years later, I understand, and his response runs through my mind

when I am exhausted. When I'm low on sleep, the fruit of the Spirit in my life, such as patience and self-control, can be in short supply.

God shows up and works his plan on my behalf when the time is right. Sometimes circumstances need to play out in others around me first.

I'm weak. I can't do this on my own. It's all about what God is doing.

Because I kept coming to the end of what I felt I could do, I was able to hear God's guidance in ways I'd never been able to hear it before. I developed a sensitivity to his voice and that he would communicate with me. He gives me that "knowing," and I know what I should do.

As T. D. Jakes says, "God exercises His grace by allowing us to ferment in the supposed stillness of transition so that we might be ready for the next stage."[1]

Thank you, Lord, for making a change in me during this waiting

---

1   T. D. Jakes, Crushing: God Turns Pressure into Power (Nashville: FaithWords, 2020), 157.

time. As crushed grapes change in the resting process of fermentation, so the fruit of the Spirit and gifts you have given me grow for your purpose and glory.

The *resting* stage of fermentation is not really a rest, but rather more of an expected wait. In the classroom, teachers call this active listening; leaning in, watching, listening, and responding. You can do all of this without talking. For a student, this is a time of engaged learning and expanding knowledge as they assimilate new concepts and make connections with past experiences and current understanding. As a Christian, I've learned that sometimes epiphanies or shifts in my understanding have happened during these times of active waiting, like an expectant mother eagerly anticipating the new life growing inside.

Obedience can be scary, but the results are exhilarating. We feel called to foster, and when I have been obedient to what I think God is asking me to do, it is initially scary because it requires faith, time, effort, and indifference to what others will think. When I obey and take the step of faith, I find the task exhilarating! The thing I thought I couldn't do, I did! I can't say I am without fear or trepidation when I obey. Isn't that the definition of bravery and faith— doing the right thing even though it is scary? Merriam-Webster's definition of *bravery* includes "showing mental or moral strength to face danger, fear or difficulty."[2] The definition of *faith* on Dictionary.com includes "confidence or trust in a person or thing."[3] I am brave when I have confidence and trust in God.

---

2   Merriam-Webster, s.v. "bravery" (n.), http://www.merriam-webster.com/dictionary/bravery.

3   Dictionary.com, "faith," (n.), dictionary.com/browse/faith.

Often, I ask my husband, parents, or a friend for input with difficult decisions. However, sometimes there are urgent situations that require immediate responses when no one else is around. There are also times when others' counsel or opinions fall short, and we have to dig deep and decide if we should foster or adopt a particular child. God is the only one who can offer direction because he is the only one who can see the unforeseen details and outcomes.

God is the one who directed us to take these children. He has a purpose in bringing us together. He gives us everything we need each day, and somehow, that is enough. We are woven together, even though I know we will all diverge onto separate paths one day. Just as I see the little ways all of our children have grown throughout our time together, God has even bigger plans than I could ever imagine as we live and grow as a family. He shows his greatness through our weaknesses.

10

Survival Tips to Prevent Burnout for Everyone in the Family

""Return to your rest, my soul, for the LORD has been good to you."
Psalm 116:7

How I Recognize I'm Close to Burnout

Sometimes when I am happily floating down the stream of occupied, a whirlpool of overwhelmed rises out of nowhere. I find myself sputtering as I'm suddenly sucked down into over-commitment. As if in an illogical dream, I try to talk myself out of drowning as the water's force and pressure overtake me. I reason with myself, believing the shame I feel as I dialogue within my mind.

Nothing I am doing is that hard. I can do these things, and I'm good at them, so I should do them. Since the last foster children left, we have a spot available. Maybe I should say yes to the friend who has been pleading with me to consider the foster child she can't keep. The child is outside our family's comfort zone, and we should take a break to catch up on life before we have new foster children move in, but we could make it work.

I try not to guilt myself into saying yes, but this is a real struggle for me at times. Reality sets in when we are engaged in nonstop activities and I miss texts or voicemail messages telling me dates and times have shifted to collide with other plans.

It's when I hit one of these walls that I stop for a second and look at the situation. I realize I am already doing my part to help kids, and it is okay and necessary to start saying no so we can nurture the relationships in our family and keep up with previous commitments.

I want to commit to helping people and invest in activities that seem valuable or fun. But my life is busy and convoluted. I am slowly learning that the uncomfortable response—no—is better than resenting people for talking me into something I was uncomfortable with from the beginning.

I begin to recognize my need for rest when I realize that I'm not my usual smiley, bubbly self. When I get quiet or begin to withdraw into myself, I realize I need to take time for myself to prevent burnout. I take a nap, go for a walk outside, or take a break from the daily grind.

Sometimes I allow myself to purposefully ignore my messy room and never-ending tasks to pray, journal, and reflect. Calling a time-out for myself gives me a chance to stop and make hard decisions as to what needs to be shaved from my schedule when it all feels important. During a rare time-out, I might go to a women's retreat. I feel restored when I allow myself to be enveloped in God's rest.

When you feel like you are in a pit alone, don't believe the illusion. Quiet yourself before your heavenly Father and know you are loved. He sees you right in the middle of all that surrounds you. He is there with you and has been all along, even in the scary parts of life.

The things that got me through times of burnout were little, but real.

- Praying

  Lord, continue to fill me up with your joy and peace each day.

Renew my hope.

- Breathing in fresh, cold air and looking up at frosted trees or a sunset.
- Sitting by a window on a short winter day and feeling the sunshine pour over me.
- Enjoying a hug, shy smile, or belly laugh from one of my beloved first-graders.

I release my anxiety as I pray, *Lord, help me to learn this lesson quickly.* In these little moments, God communicates, *I'm here. I see you. I love you. When you come to your end is where I begin to reveal myself.*

At times, when it feels like children are doing whatever disrespectful things they want, I cry out from the chaos, *Lord, I've hit the end of me! I need you to show up here!* And he *does*! Through a student, parent, teacher, or family friend, the Holy Spirit sends the help I need at that moment.

I find that during these stressful times, I need more date nights. My husband and I sneak off to a nearby coffee shop before the kids wake up on a Saturday morning. They all know they can wake up Shariah if they need anything, but we're usually back before anyone is up. Sometimes we will walk to a local restaurant a couple of blocks from our house after we get the kids settled with dinner and a movie.

Strategies to Help Prevent Burnout

Hug!

Lots of hugs for everyone involved!

Dance!

Put on some fun music and have a dance party. Sometimes this is most needed when we're having a rough day with lots of crazy emotions and

everyone is feeling grumpy. Twirls and wiggles have a way of making smiles bubble to the surface.

Sing!

As an elementary teacher, I've discovered that children generally respond to music. The younger girls in our home like to sing. I remind them that singing or listening to music can help chase away a grumpy attitude. Singing can also help dreary chores get done more quickly.

Grace

After it's over, it's over. Once a negative behavior has been addressed, everyone says sorry and takes care of any logical consequence. All is well. No moodiness allowed, moms and dads. Sometimes I have to remind myself that attitude is a choice, and I have to consciously decide I am going to think about something differently.

Mini Coaching Reminders

Coaching and pep talks are part of parenting. As a teacher, I do this often, but I know it is always good for me to remind myself to be intentional about having teachable moments. When a child is upset, they are not open to listening. Once a child is calm or when they are in a good mood is the perfect time to talk to them individually. The shorter your side of the conversation, the more memorable it can be. For example, when a child is singing, I might say, "I love to hear you sing. You know we can choose our moods. Sometimes when I'm sad, I sing, and it helps me feel better. Next time you have to clean your room, you could try singing or listening to music instead of getting angry."

Help a Child Recognize a Negative Action When They Are Engaging in It

Children will come into your home with habits they need help breaking. Examples might include talking back, eye-rolling, cussing, interrupting, or telling adults what to do.

Frequently, children don't know they are engaging in an inappropriate habit until you talk to them about it and start pointing it out. I come up with a word or a hand signal to let them know they are doing it so they can begin to recognize the behavior. Depending on the child's intent, I have initially allowed a certain number of reminders before a consequence. Then, as the child gets better at curbing their behavior, I decrease the number of reminders before having the child serve the consequence.

Reframe Negative Thinking

Come up with little positive words to reframe negative thinking. You could start calling a grumpy child "Sunshine" or "Happy." You could post and say Bible verses and other catchphrases to refocus everyone. For example, "Do everything without complaining and arguing" (Phil. 2:14 NLT) or "Teamwork! Let's get this done!"

Positive sayings that reframe negative thinking are essential for adults too. We set the tone and atmosphere for children.

Change the Subject and Location to De-Escalate Emotional Outbursts

Sometimes escalations over petty arguments or annoyances can be diverted or dropped by a question or a change of topic and location. This tactic can work for individual children or multiple children who need to take a break from each other. For example, I have interrupted arguing children with comments such as "I think we'll go to the library today! Let's get ready," "Come help me in the kitchen while your sister finishes reading," or "Let's watch a movie!"

This distraction allows them to calm down. If I tried to talk to them right away, it would throw lighter fluid on their disagreement.

A few minutes later, as we settle into a task such as setting the table, we can talk about it briefly. "Would you like it if your sister kept bothering you when you were playing with Duplos?" (Wait for a reply.) "Your sister needs time to do things by herself too. When she comes upstairs, you need to say you're sorry for not letting her read."

Then let her do something she likes to keep her busy while you go down and talk to the other child.

Give Children Options Ahead of Time to Deal with Conflict

Over the years, I have coached children in my classroom using a posted "Kelso's Choice" poster we review regularly. It is a helpful visual for children as they learn to advocate for themselves appropriately when conflict arises. You can find it online. It is a picture of Kelso the frog surrounded by options to solve small problems.[1] I tell our kids that

there won't always be an adult around, so they need to learn how to take care of small problems themselves. Most of the issues in their world are small problems once they are in a safe home.

We also talk about telling an adult about big problems where someone got hurt or could get hurt. I also tell kids that if someone ever says, "Don't tell your mom or dad," that is when you have to tell a parent or an adult you trust.

Give Everyone a Little Space

Kids don't always recognize when to leave others alone or when they need time alone when frustrated or angry. You should talk kids through this. For example, if a child wants something from someone who is already agitated, that is not a good time to ask for it. I have coached, "When someone is mad, you need to give them space. Move away from her. After she calms down, you can ask to borrow her toy. If you keep

---

1 "Kelso Conflict 'It's Your Choice' Banner, K–5 (Portrait Orientation) (#GH5458)," Kelso's Choice, accessed August 27, 2019, http://kelsoschoice.com/product/kelso-conflict-choice-banner-k-3-portrait-orientation-gh5458/.

arguing with her, you know she will hit you."

Sometimes adults need time away too. The year I had an exceptionally challenging class, I took a much-needed time-out every day after school as I transitioned from teaching my very active first-graders to helping our kids at home with homework. I closed the bedroom door and told all our kids I was going to lie down for twenty minutes. "Do not knock on my door. I will come out when the timer goes off," I stated.

Time!

Make little snippets of one-on-one time with everyone in the family. We need to be intentional about spending time in real relationships with our spouse, friends, and kids, even if it's just having one child help with dinner while you talk. When I leave home to go to the store or run errands, I always take a different kid or combination of kids. Frequently, it has to do with who is nearby when I'm getting ready to go or who volunteers the quickest.

Be Fully Present and Limit Technology

You do not have to be on call twenty-four hours a day when a text or email comes in. You do not have to answer a call when you are eating dinner as a family. If you have a hard time ignoring Instagram or Facebook notifications, put your phone on airplane mode.

Refrain from checking your email when one of your teenagers takes a break to say hi or ask how you're doing. Those are times that deserve undivided attention because they can become less frequent as kids get older. Don't let technology's false sense of urgency distract you from the more meaningful moments in life with the people you love.

I learned this lesson when our teenage son stuck his head in our room one evening and said, "Hi, Mom. How was your day?" I was in the middle of checking email, and I distractedly said "Good" as I finished my email. When I looked up, he was gone. It is not a regular thing for our son to seek me out just to see how I'm doing. I felt horrible. I realized then that I need to be intentional about acknowledging him by stopping to look at him so he feels valued and I don't miss out on opportunities to connect.

What Makes You Smile on the Inside?

Make a list and be intentional about incorporating these things into your life regularly. Your list might include . . .

- Listening to your favorite song
- Watching your kids play
- Looking at a picture of a happy memory
- Drinking a cup of coffee or tea with a friend
- Calling your mom or dad
- Hugging your spouse and saying how much you appreciate who they are
- Snuggling your cat or petting your dog
- Smelling fresh flowers on your table

Go on Mini Adventures!

Mix it up—sometimes take a few kids at a time, the whole family, or just the adults. These adventures can last an hour, overnight, or an entire weekend.

- Stop at a local park you haven't gone to yet.
- Go for walks in different places as a family.

- Explore hiking trails in the area.
- Visit a friend for the weekend.
- Sign up for a paint party.
- Rent a state park cabin (they are affordable).
- Stop for ice cream at your favorite local spot.
- Go to a play place for dessert or meet a friend and her kids there.
- Go kayaking or boating.
- Sign up for a church Bible study. The kids can play with other kids while you laugh, cry, and connect to others who can pray for you.
- Visit a local garden center or greenhouse and let the kids each pick their favorite vegetable, flower, or houseplant.
- Visit a local farm to pick produce.
- Have everyone grab their swimsuits and find a place at a local pool, pond, river, or beach to swim and have a picnic.
- Go to the farmers market.
- Visit the local pet store.
- Have a picnic and watch a movie in the living room.

- Send the kids fishing with your husband while you get a massage or pedicure.
- Go to the library and check out the free kids' events.
- Observe local wildlife. Watch birds, feed the ducks, or visit a local wildlife center, fish hatchery, or petting zoo.
- Go ice skating, skiing, or snowboarding.
- Stop and let the kids skip stones when you see a great spot.
- Participate in summer or winter programs or camps for free. There are often scholarships for foster children.
- Go rollerblading, roller skating, or skateboarding.
- Stop and read flyers for local events and put them on your calendar so you don't forget.
- Go camping!
- Sign the kids up for Vacation Bible School at different churches in town.
- When friends ask if your children can come over, say yes!
- Go to cultural events in the area.
- When a friend invites you anywhere, go!

Healthy Strategies for Foster Parents

- Take care of yourself.
- Make sleep a priority. My kids say I'm always tired, but I am always up hours before them each day.
- Engage in regular exercise and time outside help relieve stress.
- Supplements such as magnesium and B-complex can help take the edge off when stress is exceptionally high. I often mix half to one teaspoon of the magnesium powder "Calm" into my tea at night when I find myself not getting restful sleep. Vitamin C can help keep your immune system running well too.
- Coffee is my friend; it can push me through the day. I find that even though I still go right to sleep at night, if I have coffee in the afternoon, I wake up tired and drag myself through the next day. Listen to what is best for your body.

- Reach out to friends who will support you. I have one friend who encourages me to exercise by asking me to go on outdoor adventures with her. Different friends helped me write this book. A few other people at church prayed for me when I lacked courage or strength for the challenges of fostering.

Now I am intentional about putting events on the calendar and saying no to some activities that stress our time. When being busy crowded out house cleaning for a week and a friend asked if I wanted to go for a hike to pick berries, I had to pass. Even though I wanted to go berry picking, I reminded myself that I needed to make time to clean the house or I would start getting frustrated with everyone. I'm predictable in this area.

The next time my friend called to see if we could get together, I said, "I need a break, and I want to see you! Can we meet for a thirty-minute walk in an hour and a half? I need to work on my book today."

"Bring your kids," she replied. As I walked onto the local high school track toward my friend, Ezra gently touched her son's arm and said, "Tag. You're it," and jogged off. All our kids ran after him onto the football field.

I've said no to requests to sing on the church worship team during high-stress times or when my husband calls a family "time-out" to go camping for the weekend. At times, I've chosen to opt out of school events as a parent and as a teacher. Most people didn't notice I wasn't there, and we got the family time we all needed. You need to work downtime into your schedule to rejuvenate yourself and connect with the people who are most important to you.

How could you combine your errands or be more productive with your time? I know I need to focus when I do bills, so my husband and I tend to work on them when the kids are sleeping or playing outside.

Get Together with Other Foster Families

Nothing can compare to connecting in person with other foster families. When I feel stressed out and like I need help, my self-talk starts sounding like this: You chose this, so you can't complain about stress.

I need to express what I am going through with someone who understands the attachment to foster children and the need for a break at the same time. As I listen to other foster parents share their stories, I realize that I could have it a lot worse than I do. Sometimes other parents help keep things in perspective by telling me our children are still adjusting from their trauma.

Arrange for Respite

Respite is where you have your foster children stay overnight with another family so you can have a break. Find a family you are comfortable with caring for your foster children. You can always ask friends for recommendations if you don't know of anyone yet.

In Iowa, we had a certain number of respite days a year. We had to arrange this through the caseworker so the respite family could get paid through the state. In Alaska, we make these arrangements on our own and pay the family directly.

If it is the first time our children are going to stay overnight elsewhere, we tell them something interesting about the family or share something fun they are planning on doing with them. If we do fun things while they are away, we are honest when children ask what we did, but we don't expound on details that make them feel left out. We ask about their time at their sleepover too.

Read Books That Encourage and Inspire You

I am too busy to sit down and read many books, but most local libraries have a program where you can download audiobooks for free. I use Hoopla, Overdrive, and sometimes Audible to listen to inspiring books when I'm getting ready for the day, driving to work, or completing a mundane task, such as laundry or cleaning out a closet. It helps me keep working and inspires me along the way. There are many free podcasts you can listen to as well.

Books Specifically about Foster Care

These varying perspectives and experiences in fostering helped me realize that, yes, fostering is hard, but it's worth my energy.

- *Faith & Foster Care: How We Impact God's Kingdom* —Dr. John DeGarmo
- *Stretch-Mark My Heart: Building Our Family through Adoption One Child (or Two) at a Time* — Niki Breeser Tschirgi
- *Faith to Foster* — TJ and Jenn Menn
- *Another Place at the Table* — Kathy Harrison

Other Books That Have Encouraged and Influenced My Thinking

- *Craft a Life You Love: Infusing Creativity, Fun & Intention into Your Everyday* — Amy Tangerine
- *Of Mess and Moxie: Wrangling Delight Out of This Wild and Glorious Life* — Jen Hatmaker

- *Reshaping It All: Motivation for Physical and Spiritual Fitness* — Candace Cameron Bure
- *How Successful People Think: Change Your Thinking, Change Your Life* — John C. Maxwell
- *Facing Your Giants: God Still Does the Impossible* —Max Lucado
- *Outliers: The Story of Success* — Malcolm Gladwell
- *The Tipping Point: How Little Things Can Make a Big Difference* — Malcolm Gladwell

Read Books That Will Inspire the Children in Your Life

When we help others, it encourages and lifts us too. Some books that we have enjoyed reading with our kids include P.K. Hallinan's books *Let's Be Happy, Let's Be Helpful, and Let's Be Patient.*

Listen to Songs That Inspire You

I found that in pivotal moments in fostering, God gave me songs that kept me afloat when I was adrift in the vast ocean of loss. Those seasons were temporary, but at the time, the sea stretched in every direction, as far as my eyes could see. These songs were a life raft to grab onto for a time. They didn't solve anything, but they offered me a thread of hope. I felt God's presence, and I knew he saw me in my desperate place.

- "Blessed Be Your Name"—Matt Redman
- "Still"—Hillary Scott & the Scott Family
- "Compass"—Lady A

To this day, every time I hear these songs, they seem written for me. I remember again that God is faithful. He was constant during that time, he is with me now, and he will guide and provide for me in the future. These songs sometimes evoke spontaneous tears even now and a strong sense of God's nearness. He was present in loss and he brought us through it.

Other Songs God Has Used to Sustain Me

- "Good Good Father"—Chris Tomlin
- "When You Walk Into the Room"—Bryan & Katie Torwalt
- "I Have This Hope"—Tenth Avenue North
- "Shine On Us"—Bethel Music & William Matthews
- "Broken Prayers"—Riley Clemmons
- "I Will Rest"—City Harbor

Songs God Has Used to Energize and Inspire Me

- "Rescue"—Lauren Daigle
- "Confidence"—Sanctus Real
- "You Are Loved"—Ellie Holcomb
- "Wonderfully Made"—Ellie Holcomb
- "While I'm Waiting"—John Waller
- "Called Me Higher"—All Sons & Daughters
- "Multiplied"—NEEDTOBREATHE
- "Mighty"—Beckah Shae
- "Everywhere I Go"—Tim Timmons
- "Lights Shine Bright"—TobyMac and Hollyn
- "Prophesy Your Promise"—Bryan & Katie Torwalt

11

Our Daily Drama

"So let's not get tired of doing what is good. At just the right time we will reap a harvest of blessing if we don't give up." Galatians 6:9 (NLT)

Pressure in our home built as emotional outbursts from the girls increased. Ava would not listen to my husband, and she did not respect him. Madison's FAS (fetal alcohol syndrome) was becoming more noticeable. She was impulsive and required so many reminders to do anything that it was thoroughly exhausting. We needed a break. My body was feeling the effects of the accumulated stress. I had a pressure headache that felt like an impending migraine for twelve days.

Notes from My Journal: The Story Continues

One morning

The morning was beyond stressful. Ava woke up whiny and didn't want to wear the clothes she set out the night before. As I stopped in her room to make sure she was getting dressed, she was putting on another outfit. I picked up her coat to help her get it on, and she protested, saying, "I want to wear a dress!"

"We don't have time to change again. Here, put your arm in," I said, holding up her coat.

She threw herself down on the floor and began to cry and holler, "I want to wear a dress!"

After she refused to put her coat on, I said, "You can walk to the car, or I will carry you to the car. If we don't leave now, your sister isn't going to get breakfast at daycare before school."

She continued to protest. "I don't want you to carry me! I want to wear a dress!"

"If you don't get up, I'm going to carry you," I said calmly.

"I want to wear a dress!"

Without saying anything more, I picked her up and carried her toward the car. She began kicking and clawed three-inch scratches on the back of my hand with her nails. As I walked, blood dripped from my hand onto the floor. I put her in her car seat and showed her my hand. "Ava, you hurt me!"

When I turned around, Madison looked scared and started sobbing. "Are you going to get rid of us now because Ava is being mean?"

My heart raced. I walked across the width of the garage and grabbed a washcloth from the top of the dryer and pressed it to my hand. Madison followed me. "Honey, life is more complicated than that. I love you." I looked away as I tried to choke back tears through my words and I hugged her tightly.

"I love you too, Mom. I don't want to have to move."

There is no lack of drama in our house!

For weeks after that, Madison was fearful about everything that her sister did, and she came to me saying things such as, "I want to stay here. I don't want you to get rid of us."

I hugged her and told her we didn't get rid of children because they misbehaved. Sometimes Jerry and I argued, and sometimes Ezra or Christianna didn't do what we asked them to, but we didn't get rid of each other. I told her that God brought them into our lives, and I was glad we got to be a part of their journey. Their mom was still trying to get them back, and God knew what was best for them.

Later the same week

We started the morning with Ava crying, saying she wanted to stay home because she was sick, a recurring theme since she had stayed home sick a while ago. She wailed for thirty minutes and refused to get dressed. "My eyes are red. I can't go to school. I have a cough and my throat hurts!" I reminded her that our neighbors invited her over that night, and she couldn't visit them if she was sick. "But I can't stop crying! I can't go to school!"

Two weeks earlier, I had taken Ava in to see a doctor, and he gave her drops for irritated eyes. Today her eyes and everything else were irritated! "I have special drops to make your tears go away. Lie down on the couch," I pointed downstairs. She laid down. I gave her the eye drops and, after a short protest when the drops hit her eyes, she stopped crying.

"Look, Mom, I'm not crying." She smiled. You never know what will work!

At the end of the week

One day I found myself asking, "*Lord, do I need antidepressants? I feel so irritable and emotional. I know that I can handle individual challenging behaviors at school and home, but overall I'm not coping well."*

After another challenging day of defiant behaviors at school, I felt numb. I didn't want to go home yet, but I didn't know where to go. I found myself driving to the library. *Maybe I'll see if there are any books on foster care.*

I don't remember the title of the book I picked up, but I flipped through it and found myself looking at the chapter about the cycle of grief that comes when a child moves out of the home. Words practically jumped off the page at me: "Irritability . . . feelings of loss . . . anger . . . sadness . . . crying . . ."

The realization hit me: I'm going through the grieving process, just how I grieved when the doctors told us my grandma didn't have long to live.

I didn't need antidepressants. This was part of the grieving process. Just knowing that my rolling emotions were natural made me feel a little better. I was still exhausted, but it helped. This was part of the cycle of fostering. I began to realize, consciously, what I had started to process subconsciously: it was time for the girls to move on to another home.

Our attachment to the girls made this decision process confusing, especially since Child Services was not imposing the move on us. We have struggled with the decision to adopt a few times in our life journey. Yet with each child, deep down, beyond the emotion of what I wanted, I knew whether we were supposed to adopt them.

Madison and Ava were placed with us because we were open to adopting if it turned out to be a good fit for everyone. While the girls were headed toward adoption, I know they were not supposed to be ours. I had to stop arguing with myself.

The following week

I grew more aware of Madison's forgetfulness and other subtleties of her FAS that I hadn't connected with the disability when she first moved in, including her impulsivity to do dangerous things. Madison liked playing with fire, climbing up on things, or climbing down to the edge of a stream when an adult looked away briefly. She often forgot her homework. Madison lost many things, including three coats and her glasses, which she normally never took off, even when she was sleeping. She feared she would need them to protect herself if something or someone woke her up at night.

The next day

The girls were doing well at our home overall. Ava's temper tantrums were not as frequent or as long as they used to be. She went to bed without complaining or crying and fell asleep within fifteen minutes. Madison didn't have nightmares projecting the realities of her past terrors into the future anymore. All our kids played together well. Madison still did things to annoy the other kids intentionally. Madison and Ava were still overly sensitive to each other and over-reactive, but they seemed happy in between all of that. Maybe this could still work. They could be so endearing

and fun. They had been to so many homes, and other parents probably wouldn't have the patience for their negative behaviors.

A couple of days later

I jerked awake from a dead sleep at 2:00 a.m. to crying and screaming. My heart jumped. Ava stood beside the bed with her face right in mine, wailing. I thought she must have had a bad dream or was sick.

Ava cried, *"I want to watch a movie!"* After returning Ava to bed three times and listening to her scream and slam doors, I found myself yelling, *"Go to bed!"*

Just the day before, a coworker had said, "You're still smiling, so it can't be that bad." I've never had a quick temper, but you can't reason with a child who shocks you awake with an unreasonable request in the middle of the night. We all had to get up and go to school in a few hours.

I know they are challenging, Lord, but I hope you have someone who will love and cherish them as their own.

The next week

Most children take for granted that their parents will always be there and keep them safe if they are scared. They don't usually worry about where they will live either.

The girls wanted to live with their mom, but Madison was also afraid of living with her. Madison had mentioned a couple of times that she was afraid of bad men finding them with their mom. She often prayed for her mom's safety.

The following day

I always think I'm okay. Since I decided to do foster care, I shouldn't need to ask for help. I suddenly found myself at my breaking point. Hours before we left to go out of town for the weekend, my husband called me at work, frustrated with the girls' fighting. I struggled for about ten minutes before I gathered the courage to ask another foster family if they would be willing to take the girls for a couple of nights to give us a break on short notice.

I am not Super Mom or Super Foster Mom. I needed respite! Thank you, Lord, for foster parents who understand! The other foster family was newly licensed, and they were excited to have the girls come over. The girls were excited to have a sleepover with the family's daughter, who they had met last week.

That weekend

I woke up and read my Bible first thing.

"So, chosen by God for this new life of love, dress in the wardrobe God picked out for you: compassion, kindness, humility, quiet strength, discipline. Be even-tempered, content with second place, quick to forgive an offense. Forgive as quickly and thoroughly as the Master forgave you. And regardless of what else you put on, wear love. It's your basic, all-purpose garment. Never be without it" (Colossians 3:12–14 MSG).

I needed that, Lord. I can picture this verse. Help me to live it out. Whatever negative behaviors come out today in the children in my life, help me to forgive quickly and love well.

The beginning of the week

Christianna's middle name, Joy, fits her perfectly. She is my sweet smiley child. But this morning, she came upstairs crying so hard I couldn't understand what she was saying. She had her hand over her cheek. "What happened?" I asked as she came upstairs. This was one of those rare cries that made me think we might need to take a trip to the emergency room.

I had to have her repeat herself because she was crying so hard. "Ava scratched my face when I told her to put her pj's away." I pried her hand off her cheek, and there was a white scratch rising up into a welt down the length of her cheek. Still having scabs on my hand from Ava's scratches, I knew just how much this kind of injury hurt, and rage coursed through me as I took deep breaths on my way down to her room. "Ava, you will *not* hurt people! You are in time-out!" I put her on the time-out chair at the kitchen table.

Lord, have mercy! As my heart raced, I thought of how teachers and principals I had worked with had commented that I was always so calm in managing my classroom. I did not feel calm right then.

A couple of long days later

Ava made me smile. She asked Christianna to make her a sunny-side up egg. Then, when Christianna gave it to her, she said, "Mom, my egg is slobbery. Eww!"

The next afternoon

I was overwhelmed with the stress of children's negative behaviors at home and school. My hope was like a helium balloon that slowly sagged closer to the floor each day. I found it hard to rally my spirits and give myself pep talks. One day I reached out to another teacher. "Tell me we can do this." I felt close to tears.

One quiet morning

Last night we had a prayer time at church. I wept a deep, emptying kind of cry. The pastor said he felt we should pray for people who believed there was no hope. It seemed as though he was talking to me; I could not see an end to the challenging behaviors of the children in my life.

At church the next day, our daughter's band teacher said she wanted to pray for me. "I keep feeling God chose you for this. He picked you for your challenging class and the girls living with you."

Other people told me we were giving the girls what they needed for that season of their lives. When I am struggling with being balanced myself, I remember that it is my responsibility to take care of the family God gave me.

A couple of days later

How Madison could stretch doing her homework or loading the dishwasher over two hours was beyond me. She could easily have done each of those tasks in fifteen to twenty minutes.

It was not uncommon for Madison to take over forty minutes and more than ten reminders to get dressed for school. Offering incentives didn't work. After an hour of reminders, when we needed to get out the door so she wouldn't miss breakfast at daycare, my patience would evaporate. I would find myself raising my voice, ordering, "Put down that string," or the many other random little toys, candy wrappers, pen caps, and so on that materialized in her hands.

Ava loved to sing and dance around the house and say, "Mama, I love you!" at least ten to twenty times a day. Both girls were grateful and would say, "Thank you for making me dinner, Mom. I like salad."

But still, I found myself getting frustrated with Madison. The constant reminders over and over with everything in her life were exhausting. Her whining at the other children wore on my patience. Both girls were calmer and did not overreact.

Madison's need to kiss my cheek and hug me once or twice every time I left the house, and often three times before bed, was exhausting and honestly annoyed me. I understood her to need to feel loved, but I would tell her that she didn't need to hug me again because she already said goodnight and I didn't like hugging that much. She was very assertive and would say, "It's just a hug. I want another hug," and she would start to give me one more. At times

I held her away and said, "No. If someone says no, you need to respect them, and you don't hug or kiss them."

Bedtime and getting ready for the day were stressful times because the girls fought with each other. I had Ava start preparing for school in the bathroom with me while I did my hair in the morning. It was like magic.

"Good morning, Mommy!" Ava began chirping happily. She was ready to leave the house in ten minutes! I saw I had left my mug in the car the day before, so I told the girls, "Get your seatbelts on, I'll be right back." I walked across the width of the double garage, opened the back door, and put the mug on the counter. When I returned and opened the car door, the four-year-old was leaning over the middle seat with her face an inch from her eleven-year-old sister's face, yelling at the top of her voice, *"I am bigger than you!"* and her sister was yelling back at the top of her lungs, *"No you're not! I'm bigger!"* The girls still couldn't be left alone together.

It helped to go to play therapy with Ava. As I shared struggles with the therapist, she understood and told me, no, I wasn't making a big deal about nothing. The parenting I was doing was challenging. She gave me strategies to try to make life better for the girls and our family as a whole. Some of her advice included verbalizing children's emotions for them when they were unable to do it for themselves. "I know you miss your mom." Verbally narrating what was happening when a child was getting upset could help a sibling know you aren't hurting their little sister. Narrating could also help a child from imposing past trauma onto current situations. "You're okay. I'm not hurting you. I am trying to help you get your shoes on." The therapist pointed out that it couldn't feel good for Ava to throw a tantrum for hours. I never thought about that perspective.

When Children
Need to Leave

"Mercy, peace and love be yours in abundance." Jude 1:2

Out of the thirty-eight foster children we have had, most of the children were able to move in with one of their family members while a parent worked toward getting them back. Sometimes the family member they moved in with was the concerned person who reported their situation to Child Services.

Although a much higher percentage of children ultimately return to their parents, we only had five children go back to their parents from our home. We have been fortunate not to have to release a child back to a family where we feared for their safety.

I was excited, along with the children, as they reunited with their families. We sent the children home with prayers and hope for their future. God brought each child into the world through their parents with specific inherited traits to fulfill his purpose through their life. Every child should be able to be raised by their parents if it is safe.

There are other reasons children left our home. One child we were comfortable fostering was moved to a psychiatric hospital after a few incidents at school when staff feared for everyone's safety. His behavior at school was an indication that he had more issues than we could address, but we did not see those issues in our home.

We asked Child Services to find a new home for children four times. Each child and situation is more complicated than one or two behaviors. If you don't know your limits, fostering will help you identify them.

As I've shared the story of Ava and Madison, know that they were not the typical experience. They were one of the most challenging placements we had. Surprisingly, the biggest initial concern (that our kids might see Madison masturbating) was not an issue in our home. She was so busy keeping up with what all the kids were doing that we did not see this behavior once. She was always quick in the bathroom too.

We had a teen for a short time who had been in a homeless shelter for a couple of weeks. We don't usually take teens, but Christmas was a week away. Reena sounded as though she had a lot of needs, and she was on meds to help calm her emotions. The caseworker was trying to find an appropriate treatment facility with room for Reena, and she couldn't give me a timeline on how long she would need to stay with us.

I couldn't leave a child in a shelter over Christmas. I told the worker that we would take her for now and see if we could make it work. We were told to call the police if she ran away and then to let Child Services know. "She's a runner," her worker explained. *Okay,* I thought with a deep breath.

Reena was kind to everyone in our home but made sure she told all the caseworkers we encountered that they let her out of treatment without going through half of the steps. From the second or third day she moved in; she began asking me to drop her off at the teen shelter. She was used to being under very structured care in a treatment facility or doing what she wanted in the shelter.

In between times of fixation, when she begged me to buy her cigarettes or take her to get weed, we actually had fun. We made cookies, watched movies, volunteered at the food bank, and went Christmas shopping. About every other day she asked to talk to me, or I had to speak to her about new issues beyond my experience: cutting, bulimia, and sexting came up in the two weeks we had together.

Our children liked having her around, but our oldest daughter was more aware of the issues. She said it was intimidating at times because Reena was unpredictable.

"When she said she wasn't going to take her medication or she talked about running away, it made me uncomfortable," our teen confessed.

We have a filter on all the kids' devices, and they know if they type something questionable or search inappropriate things, we will be sent a text. One night, Reena had an emotional explosion when I asked her about an inappropriate text. I ushered all the kids into the basement to watch a movie, and the younger ones didn't realize anything was going on.

Although I didn't think she would hurt me, she was volatile, and I didn't want the kids to get scared. In her raving, she threatened to hurt herself. She was like an enraged, caged lion, and I was scared. I was very thankful that the caseworker's supervisor answered the phone after regular office hours and took the brunt of her anger for me while I went to a different level of the house to give her space.

After the big blow-up when Reena calmed down, I asked if she wanted to get some ice cream to get out of the house. She apologized for getting so angry, and we talked about the incident briefly. She explained she wasn't ready to be in a foster home and wished she could have come to us later after she finished treatment. "You're a really good family," she said.

At the time, I told her I would talk to the supervisor and see if we could get her into a treatment facility. She said she could go back to the shelter, which is what she had been asking all along. I was glad we were able to give her a home for Christmas. We really did have a fun Christmas and many meaningful conversations. Ultimately, safety in our home is our first priority. I'm not a counselor, and she needed more support and supervision than we could give. The supervisor was my lifeline that night when I was home alone with the kids. She arranged a meeting the next day, and Reena got excited when she talked to a director from a youth treatment facility that she hoped she could return to. She was moved the following day.

When we moved across the state, Reena needed to stay in the area for visits with her mom. So I let the caseworker know two months ahead of time so she could find a good home for her. I called and asked the caseworker multiple times if she had found a home. She answered, "Not yet," a few times, then quit returning my calls.

Two days before leaving, I was beyond frustrated with the worker. I left a message, "We are moving across the state in less than forty-eight hours! If you don't make arrangements for our foster daughter, we will be leaving her at the police station because Child Services is closed this weekend!" The worker called back a few hours later and said the new family would pick her up the next day.

If I had reached out to other foster families, they would have told me to call the caseworker's supervisor until I got hold of someone to help. At the time, I didn't have the support I needed. The stress of selling, then buying a home, moving with a baby and a toddler underfoot, and trying to wrap up foster care was consuming.

Every child deserves someone to cherish them so that the very thought of them evokes a smile radiating from the heart. I had that love for the injured baby I picked up from the hospital. We spent a year cuddling and loving Eli through injuries, surgery, formula intolerance, and reactive attachment disorder. We wanted to keep him. Then God revealed to me he was not ours to keep. I was to give him to another family. The caseworker was shocked we weren't going to adopt him. It was then I learned what it was like for a birth parent to sign away parental rights, because I knew another home would be better for him. He had so many needs, and he was the same age as my content, little Ezra, I didn't get to hold as much as I wanted to. But releasing him ripped my heart out.

That beautiful clear day in the city, I needed a place outside where no one would see me. I drove to a large, rolling cemetery. I held Eli desperately, protectively, as a primal, gut-wrenching cry overtook me.

God, you see beyond the chaos of our emotions. You see that this precious baby is more than I can handle.

Once I knew I could love another child as my own, I never wanted to adopt if I didn't feel the same toward the adopted child as I felt about our birth children. One mom who adopted told me many people are looking for the perfect match for children when there are no perfect parents. She adopted girls, and one of them was twenty when she adopted her. "Every child needs a parent who will wish her happy birthday. A parent who will call because they care about her, not because they want to ask their child for money.

I have been married for twenty years, and I still call my parents to pray for me when I am anxious or need advice. I can't imagine transitioning into the world of adulthood without the safety net of parents I know I can call in the middle of the night if needed.

If a placement is not working, you can request a new home for your foster child. Ten days' written notice is customary unless an incident occurs that necessitates an immediate removal. It takes time for a child to adjust and work through the stages of grief over living without their parents.

I found that play therapists, the GAL, or the CASA worker can be supportive in helping decide to move a child. I would caution you not to say too much to a caseworker until you are sure you are going to move a child. When they make a decision, it may happen fast, and you might not know until the last minute. It is not unheard of for a caseworker to call and ask to have a child ready to move in twenty minutes although we usually know a couple of days to a week in advance.

Notes from my Journal: The Story Continues

Before Court

As the next date for the termination hearing approached for Ava and Madison, I had a growing need to decide whether we would adopt them. I knew the girls had to be in a home for six months before they could be adopted. If we weren't going to keep them, they needed to move to a family who might want to adopt so they wouldn't have to wait any longer than necessary.

I stopped at the bank on the way to pick the girls up from daycare. I looked up and saw an adorably quaint church with a cross illuminated below the steepled bell tower. From behind the church, a glorious sunset radiated up in a yellow glow, flushing the clouds pink. The colors filled my soul with peace.

"Now may the Lord of peace himself give you peace at all times and in every way. The Lord be with all of you" (2 Thessalonians 3:16 NIV).

One spring day

We met with the girls' caseworker and told her we decided that we could not adopt them. She asked if we could keep them until summer—six months away—while a relative got a foster care license. That seemed an eternity away. We felt it was vital for them to move before the placement became unhealthy for everyone.

The next day

We put in a thirty-day notice to find another home for the girls. Surprisingly, it was a wonderful week, positively mellow.

Ava was sick. She snuggled up close as we watched a movie. I kissed the top of her head and wondered how I could let her go to another family. So many things could go wrong, but I had to trust the girls were resilient and God loved them more than I did.

I don't know how to explain it except to say they felt like nieces rather than daughters. But I would miss them.

Why was my heart so fickle?

Eighty-five to ninety percent of the time, Madison and Ava were affectionate and sweet, but the ten to fifteen percent could be so intense.

During warm moments, I would think, *Why can't we make this work? They are kids. Every child is challenging at times.* However, I couldn't deny the lack of sleep from anxiety and the reality that I was more emotional than usual. I was ready to get off the mental roller coaster of questioning myself.

Lord, it is scary to surrender the girls to the unknown. They were yours before they came to us. You love them. I feel as though we are another rejection along their path if we give them up. I will choose to trust you. We need your peace.

I wrote a message to another foster mom, saying, "We gave a thirty-day notice. Does Child Services usually put off moving kids until the end of that time frame? It's been challenging to make this decision for a lot of reasons, but the sooner they move, the easier it will be for all of us."

Her reply expressed her empathy for our struggle. "I'm sure they will wait the full amount of time you've given to try to find a home. Deciding to say no is the absolute worst. Even with our little man who is leaving today, I want to think that we should keep him here, but in the end, I know that this is good (for him and us). My schedule is crazy, and toddlers are too much for our family right now. It is heartbreaking to let go, but I also believe it is an exercise in faith to continue to cover them in prayer and know that God can do greater things than we can (even when they are not in our hands).

"I'm sure the girls love you! Of course, they are going to be torn with loyalty to Mom, even if they know she is not right for them. Sin leaves a mess behind it, and when it comes to family, it can consume. Praying for peace for you and for the girls to go to a Christian family who will be God's hands and feet for them."

A couple of days later

I was emotionally numb and physically exhausted. I was tired of thinking about the girls moving on. It would be better if it just happened.

Two days later

I decided to start counting down to the girls' meeting to change their placement. Maybe this would help me look forward to their transition instead of swaying back and forth.

People don't understand why we would put ourselves through this. As I wrote this, Ava kept coming to me for snuggles. The deepest part of me warmed with happiness. I didn't understand how I could have this love and yet be coming to a place where I was okay with the decision to let them go. They were worth every snuggle, every test of my patience, and every time I had felt straight-up anger.

I wanted the girls to feel fully loved. I wanted them to know they were not alone in this big world when they didn't know if they would get to see their mom again. They were too young to understand all the complicated reasons why each family couldn't keep them.

Lord, may they not have to keep changing homes. You know where they need to land. Please let them find a permanent home. Thank you for protecting them.

One foster mom told me, when she found out her foster daughter was going back to her mom, she signed her up for summer programs to make the transition more gradual. Intentionally providing activities to create distance made sense.

When we decided to have the girls move, I let them stay at daycare a little longer, but after two days, I realized I missed them when I went home after work before picking them up. I needed to lean into loving them, finish strong, and enjoy them as their mom until the end.

A new week

I was hopeful. The family who took the girls for the weekend said they were willing to be the girls' next placement.

While the girls were having fun with their new friends in respite, it felt so good to have the five of us squished in the car, headed out of town. I loved hearing our biological kids giggle, tease, and joke in a way that made all of us laugh.

On Sunday night, I was so excited to see the girls, and although they were happy to be back, Ava said she had a sore throat and Madison didn't necessarily light up at seeing us. That was fine. Maybe God was preparing them to move. The foster mom told me they talked to their landlord, and they are only allowed to have one more child in their home, but they would be willing to take the girls anytime we need respite. It would be such a blessing to have a break when we needed it.

As we were talking to the respite family, another couple was waiting to speak to us. They asked if our three youngest would be interested in going to their children's AWANA Bible Club with them Tuesday nights. God is so good. Another blessing.

When we got home from church, it was fun to hear the girls explain all they did while we were gone. None of us had eaten yet, so we had big bowls of homemade soup before getting ready for bed. As Ava put on her pj's, she looked down and patted her very full, extended tummy. She said, "Look, Mommy. I think I'm getting a baby."

I smiled.

The next week

I came home to Ava crying loudly in her room and my husband sitting quietly in the chair in our bedroom, trying to calm down. They had just come back from preschool where Ava had been defiant and refused to leave. My husband ended up having to carry her, kicking and crying, to the car. Ava has not been listening to him lately.

After I submitted our thirty-day notice, we gave the caseworker a week; then we called to find out when the required change was going to happen. Her voicemail recording stated she would be gone for two weeks. I asked to talk to the supervisor, and she said she would schedule the meeting the day our worker returned. I left a message the morning our worker returned to the office, asking her to call me. She phoned at lunchtime to confirm the meeting. I was excited and nervous.

A couple of days later

I prepared a shortlist of the girls' positive and challenging behaviors in case I had to speak at the meeting today. Usually these meetings happen without input from foster parents, but I wanted to share my concerns.

A half hour beforehand, the caseworker still hadn't sent me the number for the conference call. She didn't answer her phone, but I was able to get hold of her supervisor, and she gave me the phone number I needed to participate. When I asked how long the meeting usually lasted, I was surprised when she said a couple of hours. I told her I could only listen in for the first half hour, and she told me to make sure I let the facilitating caseworker know.

Sometimes I think in word pictures. Before I called in to the meeting, I pictured a door before me. With dread and a touch of anxiety, I reached forward to open the door, not because I wanted to, but because I knew it was the best thing for our family, including the girls. Ava's aggression and disrespect toward my husband and the visibility of Madison's needs were rising. We loved these girls dearly, but we could not do this forever. I called in to the meeting.

The facilitator started by asking if both birth parents knew about the meeting. The mom had changed her phone multiple times and did not respond to relatives telling her about the meeting. When the caseworker said she didn't know if the dad (in prison) was invited to the meeting. The facilitator said we could reschedule so the dad could be present.

I explained that I had given my notice three and a half weeks earlier, and it wasn't an emergency at that time, but now we were at the end of our thirty days. The facilitator said these meetings should happen as soon as possible for the department to offer support to maintain the viability of the placement. He then asked what the department could do to support us so the girls wouldn't have to change homes.

I explained that going to therapy with our younger foster daughter had made the placement last a lot longer than it would have otherwise. Now that the case was moving toward termination, it would be best for them to move to an adoptive home because we had decided not to adopt.

The facilitator said it didn't sound like an emergency placement was needed for the girls and asked if we were willing to keep them a few months longer while they found a family placement.

I was glad when the girls' caseworker said an emergency placement was needed and the girls' needs were significant enough that this was their ninth home. She added she had looked into about sixty different family members, and they were either unsuitable or unwilling to take the girls.

The next day

It was going to be a big day. I needed to start on Easter planning and then laundry and packing with the girls after that. Last night went better than I could have ever imagined.

After therapy, Madison and I had stopped at Fred Meyer's for a few groceries, and Madison helped me pick out some fresh flowers for the table. I love the smell of the daffodils this time of year. Next, we stopped to pick up Ava at daycare.

Madison ran ahead of me into Ava's classroom. As I went by the front desk, I stopped to say that today might be the girls' last day. The caseworker was coming to our home on Friday to move them to another foster home. The daycare receptionist said they require a two-week notice. I reminded her about our discussions about a possible upcoming move. I didn't know until today when the girls were going to get moved.

That morning, before our meeting, I had mentioned to the director that today might be the girls' last day. She seemed worried about Child Services not paying for the girls. I hoped we wouldn't have to pay for childcare until the end of the month after the girls moved and I hoped that the next foster family would continue daycare there. Ava loved her teacher and friends.

I was so thankful that the termination meeting happened on a Wednesday when Madison had counseling so I could talk to the therapist and have closure before the girls left.

The therapist helped me feel better about the girls moving on. After dinner that night the girls were playing in the living room and I began in a positive tone, "Life is an adventure, and everywhere we go, God is with us. He goes before us, and he protects us. Life takes us places we don't expect sometimes. We have had many fun memories together, and we will always love you. On Friday, you are going to get to move to a new family, and I heard they have kids and a dog!" I held my breath.

I expected Madison's face to fall and for her to start crying at any moment.

Ava responded first. "Yay! We're going to a different family! Do we get to sleep there? You're the best mommy! I love you."

"Yes. You get to live with them like you used to live with Ms. Kat." She was the foster mom they lived with before us.

Madison asked if they went to church, and I said, "Yes. You'll get to go to church with them." She asked a few other questions, and she seemed okay. I had expected fireworks of emotion. But she was having a normal conversation. Inwardly, I let out a sigh of relief. *God, you are so good! I could have never imagined this conversation going this well.*

I saw I had missed a call from the caseworker. No message was left. When I returned her call, she was very short and said she had found a placement for the girls and would be by between 3:00 and 4:00 p.m. on Friday to pick them up. I asked if the girls could meet the family beforehand.

"No," she stated flatly.

"Feel free to give the foster family our number if they have questions. I'd love to let them know what little things were helpful with the girls to avoid conflict." The girls were complicated.

"Just write down any notes you have."

"So you don't want us to see or have communication with the next foster family?" I was getting frustrated.

"No. Not at this time."

"Will the girls need to change schools? Do you need me to call?" I suddenly felt like I was being stranded alone somehow.

"No. I'll take care of everything. I'll see you Friday between 3:00 and 4:00 p.m."

Maybe she had had a bad day or was in a hurry, or maybe I was just too attached, but that was the worst interaction I ever had with one of my foster children's caseworkers. I was suddenly horrified. Panic grew in the pit of my stomach. What if the girls left school and never got to see their teachers and friends they loved again? What if they didn't get to say goodbye? Couldn't we at least meet the next family? We loved these girls and wanted to make sure they would be okay (not that we would have any say if we didn't like the new family). I knew the majority of foster families would want to meet ahead of time or speak to the previous foster family. Foster moms I have talked to are eager to meet their kids and would be willing to have a playdate the same day they agree to take a placement as opposed to not having any contact with a previous home.

The nature of foster care is waiting and being jerked around with stops and starts, so we are more likely to act quickly on opportunities as we're going into a placement. Child Services seems to only operate in crisis mode!

I shouldn't have worried. God went before us and amazed me with his attention to details. Even though the next family had a stay at home mom, they had the girls continue with daycare for a month to help them transition and we didn't have to pay for childcare after the girls moved out.

The next day

As the girls prepared to leave, Jude 1:2 was my prayer for all of us: "Mercy, peace and love be yours in abundance" (NIV).

Madison asked why they were moving.

"Dad and I love you both, and you didn't do anything wrong. We need a break from foster care."

"Are you going to miss us?"

"Yes. We have had a lot of fun memories together, and we love you. You know we adopted Deanna, and we miss her. We talk about her, and we get excited when we see her. We still love her even though she doesn't live with us anymore. She is part of our family. You are family too."

"What will we call you when we move?" Madison shifted on the couch.

"You can call us Robin and Jerry. I hope if you see us at the store or around town, you will come over and say hi if your foster parents let you. We will be thinking about you and praying for you." I grabbed her hands in mine and gently squeezed them as I looked into her eyes.

I found out that Madison was going to get to continue at the same school.

That night I sent an email to Madison's teacher.

....

Good morning Halie,

I wanted to let you know that Madison is moving to a new foster home tomorrow. We let her know we love her and we're excited about the new adventure she is going on with a new family. She is excited but also shed a few tears.

They are moving into a therapeutic foster home. I am hopeful that this will be a good fit for the girls who need more than we know how to give.

I found out Madison will not have to change schools. I'm glad Christianna and Madison will still be able to see each other at school. Despite all the drama at our house, the two of them are good friends.

Thank you for all your prayers.

Warmly,

Robin Hunt

....

Romans 5:6 reminds me, "Christ arrives right on time to make this happen. He didn't, and doesn't, wait for us to get ready" (MSG).

The last day

The girls were leaving. Ezra and I got up early to get a few presents for the girls while they slept. I got a picture cube to give each of the girls so they would remember their time with us and have pictures of themselves. Anything having to do with pictures always takes me more time than it should. I got lost in the memories as I looked for the perfect ones.

As we got back in the car, I mentioned to Ezra, "You know the girls have been in foster care for more than a year. They don't have any pictures of themselves from that time. They have both had a growth spurt, and Ava has changed a lot since she has lived with us. They don't have pictures of themselves growing up. Ava would have been a toddler when she first went into the system." I got emotional and was trying to hold back tears.

I have many adorable pictures of Ava and Madison. They are very photogenic. Their other foster parents might have many photos too, but either none of them went with the girls, or they were lost before they came to our home. I was always amazed at how well Madison remembered details and the names of people she met only a few times. I started to get emotional and prayed I would be able to be strong for the girls so they could move on with happy expectations instead of sadness.

When the girls had come to our home, the previous foster mom got emotional and I totally understood.

A couple of times, Madison had come home after a visit with her mom with tear tracks on her cheeks. For a while, the girls had supervised visits with their mom over the phone. I had the girls take the phone into their bedroom so they wouldn't be distracted by what everyone else was doing. I was sorting laundry outside their bedroom, and I was surprised that most of the time was spent repeating that they loved and missed each other, and there were many tears and promises to pray they would be back together soon. I didn't want our parting to look like that. I wanted the girls to know it was okay and good to have fun when we were apart and it was okay to love other people.

I was glad we had a couple of days for questions to come up. I told them on Wednesday night and they left on Friday. After we told the girls, we snuggled on the couch and watched a movie. The three youngest girls played outside afterward in the snow. I could hear the laughter as they chased each other. Every walk we ever took as a family always ended up with at least one game of tag intertwined somehow. As they played outside, I washed clothes and began packing their things. When the girls came in, they were in a good mood, and they helped me pack.

Ava came into the kitchen. I spoke to her for both girls to hear. "Remember, Ava, when you are feeling sad or grumpy, if you start to sing songs, it helps you to be in a good mood. Loving your next family is okay. I want you to love them. You are good at loving other people and being helpful too. Remember, you can choose to be in a good mood."

The day the girls left, Madison asked us again if we would miss her. "Yes," I said, hugging her. Ava happily climbed into the caseworker's Suburban to meet her next family.

It was only after they left our home that Christianna told me

Madison went to play the piano after our we told the girls that they were moving, and a couple of tears slid down her face. She asked Madison if she was excited to go to a new home, and Madison said yes.

When I saw the girls' previous foster mom in church, she asked if the girls were still with us. I told her, "They left this weekend."

"How are you?" she asked.

"I'm okay." I felt a little numb, and I didn't know what I should think or feel. "The house is quiet."

"I bet you don't miss the fighting and arguing," she replied.

"Or the crying and tantrums. But I miss the hugs and their singing and laughter."

"Oh, you don't have to tell me. I know," she replied.

And it felt so good to know that she did know. They took a part of her heart with them, and she agonized over the decision to let them move on as I did. It can be easy for a foster parent to spin the story based on all the overpowering negative highlights of the week or share all the sweet things and skew the reality for people who have not experienced life in our home.

"I never appreciated how well our kids get along," I said.

"I hear that from a lot of foster parents after kids leave," she replied.

It is so affirming to connect with other foster parents without having to explain the complicated experience. It can't be fully understood by people who haven't fostered. Like resolution on a camera, the clarity is lost. Fuzzy.

The day after

The girls left yesterday, and I decided that it was time to follow through on plans to book a cruise as a family. We had been talking about going for two years. Now that the girls were gone, we needed to slow things down and re-center our family unit. A cruise would be a perfect time-out to simplify our lives.

We spent the evening looking up cruises, excursions, airfares, and hotels. We got most of it booked.

The following morning

I woke up feeling more like myself than I had in a long time. Reading Psalm 103 renewed me.

"He crowns you with love and mercy—a paradise crown. He wraps you in goodness—beauty eternal. He renews your youth—you're always young in his presence" (MSG).

I felt thoroughly loved to the deepest part of me, like taking a warm bath after being outside on a cold, wet day. Love seeped into every crack until every part of me was saturated.

I usually listened to praise music or an audiobook before school. This morning as I got ready, I felt I should listen for what God had to say to me. I had a powerful sense I was entering a time of restoration and equipping for myself and others in foster care.

I was to write this book as a way to encourage others and acknowledge the trial-blessing called foster care. Reading other foster care books was like coming up for air when I felt I was drowning. My hope is that this book will allow others to catch a breath in the midst of their struggle and offer hope and perspective.

Lord, use this book to minister to others. I want you to be acknowledged through this journey we are on.

The next afternoon

I deleted play therapy two days a week from our regular schedule. Ahhh, the feeling of lightening my schedule was refreshing. I would have so much more time for everything, especially our children. I would have more patience throughout the day too. God is so good.

One stress-free morning

This morning, as I was making breakfast before school, Shariah said, "Isn't it nice not to hear arguing every time someone breathes?" I just laughed.

A month later

We saw Ava and Madison at a school parent night! I was so excited to see them. They came over, waved shyly, and said hi. I jumped up and gave them both a big hug. "Oh, it's so good to see you!" I exclaimed. "I heard you have other kids at your house. Do you have fun playing with them?"

"Mostly," Madison replied. Her new foster sister came over then and asked if she wanted to walk around to the learning activities.

"Bye," she said before running off with her new friend. Her typical, energetic self made me smile.

"It is so good to see you Ava," I said. Ava smiled shyly, then walked back to her foster mom at the next table and sat down with her new family. My heart overflowed with love and contentment in that moment.

13

What Do Foster Parents Want Others to Know?

"I am going to do something in your days that you would not believe, even if you were told." Habakkuk 1:5b

Even though it is harder than they expected, most parents do not regret fostering or adopting. When people found out I was writing a book about fostering, many moms shared their arduous journeys with the vulnerable children God brought into their lives. I've heard stories of joy and hope that came to an end when they felt they lost their beloved child to drugs or when their love was rejected.

As a mom comes to the end of sharing a difficult journey and swipes at the tears welling in her eyes, I always ask the same question. "Knowing how hard it has been, if you could go back, would you still have chosen to foster (or adopt) them?" The answer from these brave mamas' shattered hearts is a resounding yes!

One mama told me she had a foster daughter in and out of her home for over a decade. This daughter of her heart overcame countless obstacles. They shared a beautiful, fun-loving relationship, and she was like one of their own children, even though the state repeatedly returned her to her birth mom. Then this daughter tried meth, and now she is not the same person anymore. This mama mourned the loss of the beloved daughter. The enemy had stolen her. Her daughter became verbally abusive, blaming her for everything in her life. "We gave her everything we gave our other children. The last time she was here, I had to tell her not to come back," she shared through tears.

When I asked this tender mom if she would do it over again, she jumped over my words before I could finish asking the question. "Yes! *A million times, yes!* She was like one of our children."

I agree with the moms who said they are thankful they didn't know how hard some parts would be, or they might not have fostered. Yes, all the moms I've asked would do it again, even if it turned out the same.

In seasons when we come to a desolate desert of hurt and hope is as faint as water, we are suspended. We are mamas wanting to trust God's promise that we are new every morning. Yet we don't know what to think as our hearts race within our chests. We pray, "Lord, bless our children and bring them back to you." But can we dare to hope that God can heal the hurt between us? We lost our innocence when repeated and forceful breaks in trust shattered our relationships. We want to believe, hope, and love fully without hesitation.

Lord, have mercy on us all as we discover in this place of faint hope that you are faithful.

"Because of the LORD's great love we are not consumed, for his compassions never fail. They are new every morning; great is your faithfulness" (Lamentations 3:22–23).

The truth is, we are more resilient and adaptable than we will ever imagine, and we will rise to the challenge—except for the days we don't, and we allow ourselves to feel defeated, or we are sucked into the whirlpool of overwhelmed. Those moments are real and do happen. Maybe it's because we are listening to the lie inside our head that we are not doing the best we can. Or that we could have done something better. We don't know what, but something! I love the saying "Don't believe everything you think."

You are not alone. Look around you and ask for support. Some people will support you emotionally by listening, praying, and helping out if you ask directly and make your needs known. "I'm so busy" or "I'm overwhelmed!" don't count. These phrases have become a regular part of our culture and are far too vague.

Read the chapter "I Don't Know if I Can Do This Alone" for practical ideas on finding support.

Once I began foster care, I started to encounter situations when I didn't know what to do or how I should respond in urgent situations. In moments of helplessness, God met me time after time. He gave me the self-control to go into the other room. He gave me the presence of mind when things didn't go how I planned to step back and not do anything at times.

"I'm frustrated right now. We're all going to take a break and calm down," I would say. I learned to be comfortable with letting a child have an angry cry, and I learned to allow myself to cry too.

When I know I am doing what God has asked me to do, I step out knowing he will make up the difference when I come to the end of myself. That is when I see him provide and feel his presence. When I feel the weakest, he makes himself known, and my faith grows. I trust him more.

Fostering is exhausting and scary, and takes all the mental, emotional, and physical strength you have some days. But it is also exhilarating, like making it to the end of a challenging race or cresting the top of a mountain where the world spreads out before you, and you can see in every direction. You can look back and see how far everyone has come. While you remember the difficulties, the valleys seem smaller from the top somehow. As you look ahead, you see the beauty and hope of the future. Like having a baby, it was painful but so worth the birth and struggle to raise that little one, with all the scrapes and kisses along the way. There is nothing like it and you are forever changed.

C. S. Lewis wrote in *Mere Christianity*:
I think that many of us, when Christ has enabled us to overcome one or two sins that were an obvious nuisance, are inclined to feel (though we do not put it into words) that we

are now good enough. He has done all we wanted Him to do, and we should be obliged if He would leave us alone. But the question is not what we intended ourselves to be, but what He intended us to be when He made us.

I think, before returning to foster care, I had slipped into this mindset without realizing it. Now that I have realized he can and will respond to present needs in my life, I can honestly say, "God, what did you intend me to be when you first imagined me into being? What purposes do you have for me? You have walked by me and rescued me and reassured me over and over like a parent calling to a toddler with outstretched hands, 'You're doing it. Keep coming. You can do it.'"

Lord, you have filled me when I was empty. Fill me with your joy, such a satisfying fullness. Be glorified.

14

Questions about Getting Started

"Then I heard the voice of the Lord saying, 'Whom shall I send? And who will go for us?' And I said, 'Here am I. Send me!'" Isaiah 6:8

Who Can Foster?

Children need loving adults. You can be single, married, a grandparent, or someone who has always wanted to be a parent someday.

What Are the Requirements?

- You must be twenty-one years old or older.
- You must pass a criminal background check. If you had minor offenses with the law years ago, you can be eligible for fostering if you were not convicted of a felony.
- You must have a regular source of income to support your monthly expenses.
- Your home must pass a safety inspection. Exceptions for some issues in the house can be granted if needed. You do not have to own a home to foster and children do not have to have their own room. I know someone in a studio apartment who fosters.

- You will need to be licensed through the state you live in, which usually requires taking free training classes.
- Your foster care license is suitable for the home you have inspected. If you move to a new home, you will need another inspection and a new permit issued.

Is Fostering and Adopting through Foster Care Expensive?

Dental and medical expenses are paid for through Medicaid. If parents work full time, the state will provide a stipend that covers childcare costs. If children are brought to your home without clothing, there is often a voucher you can get from the child's caseworker for apparel. Some stores offer discounts to foster children. In our state, foster parents can get a clothing voucher for up to $350 and a FosterWear card from their caseworker that offers a ten to fifteen percent discount on clothes at some local stores.

Once you get going with foster care, the modest stipend covers the children's needs, but honestly, kennels receive more money for a boarded dog each day than foster parents get paid to meet the needs of children dealing with trauma. If I were doing it for money, I would get paid more for opening a daycare in my home, the children would have easier behaviors, and they would go home at night. We foster because we want to help children. Adopting through foster care is usually free. All expenses were paid through the state when we adopted our daughter.

Some Questions I Have Asked Caseworkers

- What do you know about the child or children?
- Were they just taken into custody?

- What can I expect when the child arrives? Are they angry/scared/talkative?
- Do the children know why they were removed?
- Have they been in foster care before? How many homes? How long?
- Why didn't the previous foster home(s) work?
- Do they have any other siblings?
- Does it look like this will be a long-term placement?
- Where does the child go to school? (You have to get them to the school they are currently attending.)
- Do the children have regular appointments such as therapy, counseling, or speech you will be expected to take them to?
- Do you know some things they like?
- When are you hoping to move them?
- Do they have any negative behaviors?
- Are they on any medications? Why are they being taken?
- Do they have an IEP (Individualized Education Program) in school? (This special education plan shows you how to help a child in school and at home since supports and strategies will be listed in the plan.)

Do I Get a Say in Which Kids Come into My Home? I Don't Think I Could Take a Special Needs Child.

As a foster parent, you get to state any preferences you have regarding the age, gender, and needs of children you accept into your home. Our license states that we are licensed for three children from five to eighteen years old, and our preference is five- to ten-year-olds. Some children are considered "special needs" in foster care because they can be harder to place, not because they have special physical or emotional needs. Teenagers, minorities, or sibling groups can be considered special needs in some places or circumstances. We need parents who are willing to take sibling groups so that children do not need to be separated from their siblings at an already traumatic time.

When a worker calls from Social Services, they will ask if you have any openings, or if you are taking placements right now. When they say, "I'm looking for a placement today. Do you have any openings?" I often ask, "How old are they?" Then, if the age and gender fit with the sleeping arrangements we have and our family lifestyle, I say, "Tell me a little bit about the situation."

It is okay to say no. We do not take babies now that our kids are older and I am no longer a stay-at-home mom, but workers will call and ask anyway when they see we have an opening. It is essential to welcome children you feel good about and who fit into your family, lifestyle, and tolerance level. You should ask as many questions as you can think of if you are interested in having the child come live with you. You have a choice, and everyone wants the placement to be successful.

Respite Care

You can do respite care if you want to explore foster parenting without initially committing to fostering a child. This is an excellent way to make a difference by supporting full-time foster parents who need a break or have an emergency. You are paid the same daily rate as foster parents. In some states, this is paid directly by the state. Other states require foster parents to take care of these payments on their own out of their monthly stipend. Stipends for foster care and respite care pay for each night a child sleeps at your house.

I don't mind doing respite once in a while, and this is how I met some lovely children. This sounds bad, but I was surprised by how many healthy kids were in foster care. I don't remember thinking about it beforehand. I assumed foster kids would be challenging because they were in the system due to parental substance-related abuse. I was surprised by how many were in care because their single parent neglected them due to mental illness, depression, or a low IQ.

I had no interest in being a short-term emergency placement home. Children go to these homes right after being removed from a dangerous situation when there isn't a home readily available for them. Caseworkers then find an appropriate family member, foster home, or treatment center. Thank God he has people who are passionate about this vital role of helping children when they are initially removed from unhealthy situations and are transitioning to another placement. For me, the idea of continually revolving change in my family sounds overwhelming and outright scary. We have taken kids upon their initial removal from their parents, though.

I Want to Foster and Adopt, but I Couldn't Survive Falling in Love with a Child and Then Having Them Taken Away from Me!
All love is laced with pain as we work through conflict and the loss of people we love because of a severed relationship or death. This reality does not stop us from getting married or having children. When adults say, "I could never do foster care. I couldn't let them go," I think

the idea of a child's being abused and scared their whole life is more disturbing. It would be tragic for a child to go through childhood without being loved fully by anyone!

Are you willing to pick your way through the wreckage trauma left in a child's life to offer them love? Dig deep and ask yourself honestly if you could be the friend or loving adult a child needs. Are you brave enough to be the one person who will show a child they are loveable? Would you be willing to model and mentor a child so they can learn healthy boundaries? If you do not find yourself in a place in life where you can foster, you can support a family who is fostering.

Deanna's Adoption Day - Judge Block

If fostering is not something you think you can do, but you want to adopt a foster child, look into a Foster Family Agency and pursue a child who is already legally free for adoption. This is when parental rights have already been terminated and no family members want to adopt the child.

There is full disclosure with adoption through foster care. This means you are given access to all the records on file on the child you are adopting. This includes any medical evaluations, some information about the birth parents, and the situation surrounding your child's removal. There will still be parts of the story that are missing, but these records are beneficial in giving you background on a child. When we adopted our daughter, we were not allowed to take anything from the file room or make copies, but we were able to sit and read the records at the Child Services Office and take any notes we needed.

I Don't Know If I Could Be a Foster Parent

"So do not fear, for I am with you; do not be dismayed, for I am your God. I will strengthen you and help you; I will uphold you with my righteous right hand" (Isaiah 41:10).

- You can do it.
- You are not alone.
- It will be hard.
- It is worth it.
- You can love a child.
- You will make a lasting impact on each child even if you think they are too young to remember. You can make an eternal difference.

Conclusion

I do not expect to know the full extent of what God was doing when he placed foster children with us. I do know with certainty that they were chosen for us and us for them for the time we had them.

When children come to our home from Alaskan villages, their faces light up when they see we have Native food. Smoked salmon, geese, and moose soup are familiar. Other little pieces of culture that we are able to share, such as going to a Native dance or feast, are reassuring to them too. There are other cultural subtilties that we understand in their often reserved mannerisms and thinking too. Every foster parent has unique experiences and culture that can benefit children. You can reach children in a way that I can't. As the saying goes, big or small, there is a difference only you can make.

Fostering is a very humbling experience. It is challenging to deal with temper tantrums in the store, inappropriate behaviors at church, or challenges at bedtime. At times, it is okay not to be okay. It's okay to struggle with knowing how you are supposed to feel or what you are to think. God goes with us in every role we play in life. When I realize that I am not in control of my world, I find myself repeating, "The joy of the LORD is my strength" (Neh. 8:10).

Children get entangled in the consequences of adults' poor choices. A child is resilient yet tender like a snapdragon that continues to bloom in full color under the first snow. Let us breathe warmth on their brilliant colors each day. Every child wants to be seen, heard, and loved for who they are. They want to feel worthy of being looked at lovingly in a way that says, "You are a treasure! I love you completely, even though you aren't perfect. You are so precious to me. I'm so glad I get to know you. Just being with you makes me happy."

Victories over the damage adults leave behind can be ordinary things. It can be a child trusting you enough to let you hold them when they cry. It can be a child's growing confidence as a foster parent watches them with pride at a school performance. A small victory might be having dinner together and learning to take turns talking and listening to those around them. Being able to experience and celebrate ordinary moments can be significant in the life of a child.

Who knew that ordinary could be a victory! When a foster child saw me open our fridge for the first time, she said, "Wow! You have so much food." I am amazed by the many ways my understanding and thinking have changed since I became a foster parent.

Not all foster families are loving and caring. I have heard of bad homes. Yet I know many people in this world who are loving and caring. If these stories touch you, maybe you are one of those. Would you be willing to risk loving a hurting child? I cannot believe we are all too afraid of risking a little inconvenience. When these children have suffered so much, are we going to withhold love from them because we are afraid of getting hurt ourselves? How can we not help them?

We can all help. Foster, support a foster family, or pray. If we do not help now, this is the next wave of young adults we will pay for through public assistance. The statistics of homelessness and crime concerning foster children who are not adopted and age out of foster care is staggering. These vulnerable children desperately need you. You can make a lasting difference in the stability of a child physically, emotionally, and spiritually.

While fostering may not be for everyone, we are all commanded in scripture to care for the widows and fatherless. The ways to help are numerous. Buy gas for a single mom or take her son fishing. Invite a widow over for dinner or mow her grass. Give a foster family a gift card for pizza or ask a couple of their kids over for the afternoon to give the family a break. Pray for any of these people in your life and listen to their stories, and you will see ways you can meet their current needs.

My parting prayer and encouragement for you on your unique journey to change the life of one or more of these precious ones is this: "The LORD replied, 'My Presence will go with you, and I will give you rest'" (Ex. 33:14).

Book Group Guide

I'm so excited for what God will reveal to you as you participate in this study! There is a beautiful unfolding that happens when we come together with others to seek God. When we make space in our lives to stop and reflect with people on similar journeys, we learn unexpected things about ourselves. I've been amazed by things I've learned about myself and hurts I didn't know I still carried. These hidden burdens can be released by sharing them and praying for God's healing.

This short list of questions is a starting point you can use for each chapter. These are suggestions I find helpful in small groups. If one question takes up your whole time or inspires a different line of discussion based on the needs in your group, feel free to deviate. There are no set guidelines here. At the end of each meeting, I strongly suggest stopping to ask God what step you need to take next. Then write it down, pray about it, and watch for God's response in the coming days. May God bless your time in his presence. He wants to work through your life and reveal himself to you.

Be Brave & Love Well,

Robin LaVonne Hunt

Chapter Questions

1. What can you relate to in today's chapter?

2. Did this section raise any questions for you personally or about this process?

3. What truth or example can you use from this chapter? Sometimes these lessons might even be how to approach situations differently.

4. Did you find a particular story or situation daunting?

5. Sometimes we are our own worst critic. What are some things you are doing well right now?

6. What are some things that have inhibited your focus on the most important things this week? What steps could you take to avoid distractions this week?

Closing

Ask God, "What step can I take this week to support our foster journey or a family around me in need?" Allow a minute of silence to listen. Maybe a family or person will come to mind, or you might think of a need in your own life. Perhaps you already had a concern you have been thinking about before you came today. Please write it down to post in your home or put in your reminders on your phone.

Share your action step with the group or ask one person in the group to pray with you about your concern(s).

Close in prayer.

---

* To recive a study guide with book excerpts visit BreathingthroughFosterCare/com

Thoughts about
Breathing through Foster Care

A must-read for anyone considering becoming a foster parent! Hunt has the heart, fortitude, and patience for fostering children, guided by her faith in God. The wisdom she shares from firsthand experience is accurate and priceless.

~ **Kathy Berns,** *retired social worker and thirty-two-year veteran of Iowa Department of Human Services*

For those considering fostering, this book makes fostering seem possible without removing the realities. The stories are spiritually uplifting, emotionally supportive, and woven through with very practical how-to advice. As Robin shares from her personal experience and faith and offers tools that helped her family succeed in fostering, you will feel you too can answer the call to care for foster kids.

~ **Robert Aitkens,** *Life Group Pastor at True North Church and huge fan of foster families*

A lot of good life lessons. Applies to how to deal with friends and family.
~ **Abby,** *a foster cousin*

I've always wondered if I could do it myself. It is possible with the right guidance. Love how God is centered in this story. Love this book.
~ **John Moody,** *elementary school special needs attendant*

Robin Hunt is vulnerable in a way that allows the reader to feel as though a close friend has shared the deep and personal journey as well as the practical knowledge one needs for fostering children. She hasn't spared us the difficult experiences, nor has she made it sound like she's a martyr for choosing to foster children.

This book talks about real life and how to deal with the stresses of foster care added in. This book is a great read to learn about foster care from one family's perspective; a "what to expect from foster care" book. There are many nuggets in this book to help and encourage foster care families and others supporting foster care families.
~ **Elaine,** *a foster aunt*

The foster kids in the book reminded me of me. I remember acting up like that after I used to see my mom. My life is better because you guys adopted me.
~ **Deanna Johnson,** *our adopted daughter through foster care*

Robin is an experienced foster care provider over many years and with many children. She explains each stage of the process. She is especially good at communicating with the children, providing boundaries and expectations with love and care. Anyone interested in fostering can get the big picture and intimate details through this book with its challenges and rewards.

~ **Elizabeth Baker,** *foster prayer support team member*

Breathing through Foster Care gives the reader a holistic approach to foster care. As a pastor, I understand God has given each of us a head, a heart, and our hands.

Many books can be written full of information and knowledge, speaking only to the head side of our being. Some could passionately talk about the need to foster and tug on the heartstrings, propelling people to foster due to feeling bad for these children. Others could give practical hands-on suggestions to increase one's effectiveness in fostering.

I believe Robin effectively speaks to our heads, our hearts, and our hands. I recommend this book to anyone who is considering impacting the hearts of young people one child at a time.

~**Dr. Mark Zweifel,** *lead pastor of True North Church*

This book gave me the courage to move forward into foster care with excitement! Robin's transparency and heartfelt stories of fostering children gave me peace, confirming this was the direction the Lord was calling my family to serve.

~ **Kasey Brovold,** *new foster mom*

A must-read for any parent, this book shows the wonderful love, compassion, care, and perspective that children have for others. A book you will not be able to put down and can go back to for resources and the raw, heartbreaking, and heartwarming truth about attachments that last a lifetime.

~ **Alexis Rosenbery,** *child of God*

About the Author

R obin LaVonne Hunt has had a passion for children since she was a child herself. Decisions made by children can be powerful. Important decisions she made as a child range from deciding to become a teacher when she was a second-grader to deciding to adopt after completing her first big research paper on adoption as a fifteen-year-old. In their innocence, children's potential is as powerful and lasting as a redwood seed.

Growing up in a military family opened Robin up to the exciting world of other cultures in the diversity in her neighborhoods in base housing. She was one of the excited children who counted how many new kids she got to have in her class each year and grew to love change and moving.

Volunteer opportunities abroad brought her value of family and country into focus. Robin's experiences included helping build a daycare for an orphanage in Guatemala and talking to homeless children in the slums of Nairobi, Kenya about going to school. After graduating with her long-dreamed-of teaching degree, she honored her mother's pleas to "please consider teaching in the United States" when she took a job in an isolated Yup'ik village in Alaska. Kotlik is a village of about six hundred people on the Bering Sea. There are no roads in the village, and her future husband had to go home to chop ice from the river so his mom could do dishes when they were dating. Robin taught and mentored first through twelfth graders for ten years in Kotlik.

She fell in love with the generous, respectful Yup'ik culture in that village. It was there she also saw up close how some good people who love their children could struggle to meet their children's needs when they were struggling themselves. This is where her desire to help vulnerable children was born and ultimately led to foster parenting with her loving husband, Jerry.

Through fostering, Robin still gets to experience different cultures, and she wonders what lifelong decisions children might be making as they live in her home—decisions that are set firmly in their hearts to emerge like great, strong redwood trees one day . Her prayer is that these children not be broken by the storms of life and that her home could be a shelter where they can be lovingly tended so the winds of life will strengthen them.

If you have been blessed by this book Robin Hunt would love to hear from your heart, she reads all of her reviews. As a first-grade teacher and busy mom of seven, she relies on word of mouth to share her story to encourage those touched by foster care through reviews on Amazon, Goodreads, and other book reviews. Books without reviews on Amazon become invisible.

You can receive regular encouragement through her blog at breathingthroughfostercare.com where you can sign up for her newsletter. She can also be found at Breathing through Foster Care on Facebook and Instagram.

Made in the USA
Monee, IL
12 April 2021

65525091R00121